HAIRDRESSING – THE FOUNDATIONS

THE OFFICIAL GUIDE TO
Level 2

Leo Palladino

HAIRDRESSING Training BOARD

MACMILLAN

ACKNOWLEDGEMENTS

The authors and publishers wish to thank the following for providing pictures for the book:

Ian Whelpton, Clynol Hair; Brenda Rainey, Denroy International Limited (Denman); Lesley Howson and all at the Joshua Galvin Academy who kindly organised and participated in a photo shoot at the Academy; Paul Goad, Goldwell (Hair Cosmetics) Limited; Peter Hickman and staff for photos taken in the salon; Pam Goff, L'Oréal Golden Limited; Audrey Wilson and Debbie Smith, Redken Laboratories Limited; David Hill, Salon Ambience; Chris Burridge and Robert Harris, TRESemmé; Gillian Vandome, Wella Great Britain; Dr A. L. Wright, Bradford Royal Infirmary.

First published 1991 by
THE MACMILLAN PRESS LTD
Houndmills, Basingstoke, Hampshire RG21 2XS
and London
Companies and representatives
throughout the world

ISBN 0–333–55716–6

A catalogue record for this book is available from the British Library.

Printed in Singapore

00 9 8 7 6 5 4 3
00 99 98 97 96 95 94 93

CONTENTS

INTRODUCTION

Successful hairdressing depends on professional expertise and good relationships. As a successful hairdresser, you will be technically competent in your work and an effective communicator, listening to your clients and offering appropriate advice. You will have many satisfied clients who return again and again, asking for *your* services.

Hairdressing – The Foundations has been written to help you with your training. It deals not just with the facts and techniques you need to know, but also with the way you take account of the needs and wishes of your clients. This will help you not just to attain the professional qualifications available but also to carry out your hairdressing with care and confidence. Work done at this stage will be the foundation of more advanced studies later in your career.

The units in this book correspond with the syllabus of the Hairdressing Training Board. Throughout each unit there are practical activities and tips, and at the end of each unit are a checklist of the points covered and some questions to help you prepare for assessments.

The hairdressing techniques described in this book are relevant both to male and female clients. However, clients are usually referred to simply as 'she' to make the text more readable.

UNIT 04: SHAMPOOING HAIR IN PREPARATION FOR SALON SERVICES

ELEMENT 04.02: Shampooing hair in preparation for salon services

CANDIDATE NAME _____ GROUP _____

PRACTICAL OBSERVATION

a) long hair
b) short hair

	LONG HAIR	SHORT HAIR
PERFORMANCE CRITERIA	☐	☐
Positioned client's head ensuring client comfort and ease of operation	☐	☐
Controlled water flow throughout the process	☐	☐
Controlled water temperature for client comfort	☐	☐
Applied appropriate type and quantity of shampoo	☐	☐
Massaged hair and scalp using appropriate technique	☐	☐
Rinsed hair to remove all shampoo	☐	☐
Controlled the hair during the shampooing process	☐	☐
Combed to disentangle wet hair	☐	☐
Dried the hair in preparation for further processing	☐	☐
Followed safety and hygiene procedures		

Continued overleaf . . . .

WRITTEN ASSESSMENT

PERFORMANCE CRITERIA

Stated the types of shampoo available including both general and special types	☐
Explained the application of the different shampoo types to hair types	☐
Explained the massage movements appropriate to hair and scalp	☐
Explained the effects of hard and soft water on shampoo hand sets	☐
Stated the pH values of the main types of shampoo	☐
Explained how the pH of water and shampoo affect subsequent processing of the hair	☐
Explained the use of shampoo with higher and lower pH than the hair being shampooed	☐

Signed (Candidate) _____ Date _____

Signed (Assessor) _____ Date _____

Assessor's Name (please print) _____

Position _____

Hairdressing Training Board

UNIT 1

Reception

Reception – principles

Before you can so much as touch a hair on your client's head, the client needs to be received into the salon. **Reception** is the point at which the client and the salon's staff begin their relationship.

As a **receptionist** you can help relationships with clients to be relaxed, friendly and businesslike:

☆ offer a polite and pleasant greeting;
☆ give prompt attention;
☆ give correct advice and information, and do so efficiently;
☆ explain which services the salon can offer, and their benefits to the client;
☆ make sure that the client knows the salon's name, address and telephone number;
☆ quote times and costs of services;
☆ look after the client's belongings – coats, parcels, etc.;
☆ make sure that the making and timing of appointments is carefully monitored.

As a receptionist you must always be ready, available and attentive. Find time to acknowledge the arrival of each client and assure her that she will soon be attended to. Client satisfaction is one of the salon's main aims. The following points are important:

☆ Specialist hairdressing advice must be given clearly, by the hairdresser appointed to that client.
☆ Know exactly what services the salon offer. It is disconcerting to the client if staff are unsure, or cannot explain, what the salon can provide.
☆ Allow time for client consultation before hairdressing begins, to avoid any misunderstanding.
☆ However busy you are, always stay calm and unhurried – this will help you to avoid mistakes at reception.

Tip

To meet the client's expectations, offer a prompt welcome, efficient service, and attention with the minimum of delay.

☆ Create a good impression, by being well dressed and having an attractive hairstyle.

The client

Clients are essential to any hairdressing business. They attend the salon for what they may purchase. This includes not only good hairdressing, but clean, pleasant, hygienic surroundings, and well-mannered, efficient staff.

Good hairdressing is achieved by patient practice and time. The same applies to the skills required for dealing with people. Realising this is the key to success.

Disagreements and bad manners have no place in successful, harmonious working salons. The client must never be aware of staff friction, nor ever be the subject of it.

Choosing a hairstyle and treatment

Choosing or deciding exactly what is to be done can be helped by the following:

☆ Discuss with the client what she wants and expects. Further discussion between the hairdresser and client will determine the actual specialist hairdressing required – this is something the trained receptionist cannot usually do.

☆ Communicate with the client by listening to and understanding what is required. You must then interpret what is being requested and pass that information on to the hairdresser.

☆ The hairdresser will then examine the client's hair, to determine the suitability of the hair length, its state, and other factors affecting the service requested.

☆ Analyse the hair type, facial features and the like to assess whether the treatment requested is possible and safe to carry out. If it is not suitable, further discussion must take place.

☆ Advise the client where necessary. Make sure that what is finally decided is understood and that the client agrees to the service being carried out. This avoids any misunderstanding later on.

☆ Indicate how long the processes will take to complete and the cost of these services, and again make sure the client knows, accepts and agrees with these.

☆ Tests should be considered and, if possible, made before the appointment for any service. This saves time and energy.

> **Tip**
> Never attempt to carry out any hairdressing service without the client's consent.

> **Tip**
> Never bill the client for an amount that was not agreed to.

Dealing with clients

Making appointments

Each salon has its own system for making **appointments**, which should be familiar to all staff in the salon. It involves the allocation of time to be given to each client and the services requested. In general you should book services that take more time, such as perming and colouring, for the early morning or early afternoon. This allows you to fit around these services that take less time. You should also bear in mind whether the hairdresser is working alone or with assistance. A hairdresser who is preparing, shampooing, arranging products, tools and materials, and carrying out other tasks by herself requires more time for each appointment than one receiving help.

Some salons allow 30 minutes for cutting, 30 minutes for blow-drying, 15 minutes for setting, and so on. Others may allow more or less time. It is important that you know exactly how much time your salon allows, so that you can make appointments accurately and fit in as many as possible. Time wasted and mistakes in booking clients can be costly. If in doubt, check with your seniors.

ACTIVITY

With colleagues, discuss different ways of making and timing appointments. Which method is best, do you think?

An appointments system

Date: Saturday 21 September

Time	Kate	Charlotte	Sally	Sarah	David	Tony		
8.30	Jackson	Lisa			Osborn			
8.45	Wedding B/D	Wedding Put up	Beatrice	Beatrice	Wedding B/D			
9.00	Smith	Cane	Extensious	Extensious	Burwell	Morley		
9.15	CBD	P/W	Top Only	Top Only	B/D	Meche HL		
9.30	Johnstone	Jacobs			Thomas	Long Hair		
9.45	P/W	Col			Few Meche			
10.00	Williams	Meek D/C			Garner			
10.15	CBD	Cooper D/C			CBD			
10.30	Russell D/C	Cane			Meche			
10.45	Russell D/C	P/W CBD			CBD	Simmons		
11.00	Johnstone	Jacobs			Jorden	CBD		
11.15	P/W CBD	Col CBD			Semi Col	Meche HL		
11.30	Davis	Webster			Godwin D/C	CBD		
11.45		CBD	Gibbon	Grace	Semi Col	Jackson D/C		
12.00	LUNCH	Possee	CBD	CBD	CBD	LUNCH		
12.15		CBD	Jouhét D/C		meadwell			
12.30		Waldron			B/D			
12.45		CBD			Cosey D/C			
1.00	Watts	LUNCH			LUNCH	Beezer		
1.15	Meche HL					HL		
1.30			Gladstone	Crane		Jenkins		
1.45			Spiral P/W	Straightener		Top P/W		
2.00		Peters	(Long hair)	Corker	Cook	Jarvis		
2.15	John	Semi Col		Col	CBD	CBD		
2.30	CBD	Bore D/C	Payne	Straightener + Plait		Beezer		
2.45	Tyler D/C	Semi Col	S/set	CBD	Masters	HL CBD		
3.00	Watts	CBD	Selwyn D/C	Corker	P/W	Jenkins		
3.15	meche CBD	Baker	S/set + Brush	Col CBD	Tozer	P/W CBD		
3.30	Richmond	P/W	Gladstone	Jennings	HL	Gribble		
3.45	CBD	Rickets	P/W CBD	CBD	Smith	Put up		
4.00	Hobbs	CBD	Toby	Osborn	CBD			
4.15	Plait	Griffiths	Put up	CBD	Masters	Salter		
4.30	Simons	B/D		Adams	P/W CBD	CBD		
4.45	CBD	Baker	Curtis	CBD	Tozer	Sadler D/C		
5.00	Robins	P/W CBD	CBD	Stevens	HL CBD	Collins		
5.15	CBD			CBD		CBD		
5.30								
5.45								

high Hair

high Hair (Wella)

Telephone skills

Preparation

1 Always have pencil and paper to hand, so that you can make notes or take messages.

Answering the telephone

2 Answer the telephone promptly.
3 Speak clearly and directly into the telephone.
4 State the salon's name and telephone number.
5 Ask how you can help the caller.
6 Listen to what the caller says.
7 Write down the caller's name and telephone number.
8 If there is a message, write it down.
9 Complete the call by thanking the caller.
10 Replace the telephone receiver correctly when finished, so that other callers can get through.
11 Keep calls businesslike, brief and efficient.

General

12 Pass any messages on immediately or as soon as possible.
13 If you make a personal call from the salon, note how long it was, the distance you called and the time of day, so that your call can be charged to you.

Emergency services

You can call the **emergency services** – fire, police and ambulance – free of charge, at any time of the day or night. Dial **999**, then wait for the operator to ask you which service is required. State clearly 'fire', 'police' or 'ambulance', and wait for that service to be connected. When they answer, give them the full address at which help is needed, and directions to make it easy to find. Speak clearly, and listen carefully. Try not to panic – you will be able to help more if you are calm. Remember to replace the receiver properly when you have finished the call.

Other services

☆ If you need help getting through to any particular telephone number, dial **100** for **operator services**.
☆ If you can't find a telephone number in the directory, dial **192**, for **directory enquiries**.
☆ If there is a **fault** on the telephone – calls cannot be made in or out of the salon – it needs to be reported as soon as possible: any delay could be costly because a number of

> **Tip**
>
> Telephone directories, codebooks and guides to charges provide a great deal of useful information. Read them carefully, to make yourself familiar with the telephone services that are available.

```
TELEPHONE MESSAGE RECEIVED

To      Sally              Date  20.9
From    Mrs Gladstone      Time  10:30 am
Number  081-123-456        Taken by  Paula

Please could you ring Mrs Gladstone
back regarding her appointment
tomorrow.
```

A message slip

> **Tip**
>
> Never leave a telephone caller on the line for longer than a few seconds. Return to let them know what is happening. Being left on the end of a line is frustrating and the caller may hang up.

clients may be trying to make appointments. Call the operator on **151**, on another telephone line.

☆ Refer to the telephone directory for fuller information about the services available.

Taking messages

It is important to keep a written note of any **messages** you take. Use a notebook to record all messages clearly – it may be necessary to refer back to them later.

☆ Make sure you pass all messages to the people for whom they were intended. Do this immediately, and mark the message book to indicate that this has been done.
☆ If the person for whom the message is intended is not available, tell others in the salon there is a message waiting for that person. Check later that the message has been received.
☆ If messages require a reply, or if you have promised to call back, make sure this is done.
☆ Return calls as soon as possible to avoid unnecessary waiting.
☆ Listen carefully to the caller, without interrupting, and be helpful and polite in your reply.

The cost of calls is based on distance, time of day and duration of call. Keep calls short, and avoid making long-distance calls at peak time if they are not urgent.

Handling payments

When a service has been completed, you will need to calculate the client's **bill**. If you have to add up several items, double-check your answer before telling the client how much to pay.

Most salons include **VAT (value-added tax)**, which is a percentage of the total bill. This has to be paid to HM Customs and Excise – a government tax collector – quarterly, when the salon's accounts are made up. Make sure you understand the salon's method for calculating VAT, and always ask if you are unsure.

Clients may wish to pay their bills in **cash**, by **cheque**, by **credit card** or some other way. You must be familiar with all these forms of payment.

Legal tender is the name given to money that is legal to use in a country. The notes and coins produced in England, Scotland, Northern Ireland and Jersey are legal tender in the UK and may be taken in the salon. The money of Eire is not legal tender, nor is the money of other foreign currencies. There is a cost involved when exchanging it at the local banks, so you can legally refuse to accept it.

Payments by cash

1 Calculate the client's bill and double-check the final amount.
2 Clearly inform the client of the total that needs to be paid.
3 Take the client's money, count how much you have been given, and place it *on* the till, or where the client can see it.
4 Calculate the change required – use a notebook if necessary.
5 State the amount to be paid and count out the change to the client.
6 Double-check the change given and the amount taken.
7 Give the client a receipt.
8 Place the money in the till or cash box.
9 Before she leaves, make sure that the client is satisfied.
10 Check whether further appointments are required.
11 Be courteous and polite throughout.
12 Make sure that takings are recorded, so that the total day's takings can be calculated and checked against the cash in the till.

Cash registers vary from salon to salon, and may have a variety of features which deal with cash transactions. These are useful in producing receipts, totalling individual takings and salon takings, plus other features. Make sure you understand how to use the cash register. Always ask if you have a problem or if you make a mistake.

At the end of the day, record the cash register totals in a book, so that accounts can be kept. In most salons the total takings for hairdressing services and sales of other items are listed separately. Records of **petty cash** and other expenses must be kept so that the final totals can be balanced. Find out how to fill in your salon's **cashbook** accurately. Keep your entries neat and clear to read.

Payments by cheque

Many clients prefer to pay their bills by cheque. This is as good as cash if accompanied by a **cheque guarantee card**. This card guarantees payment up to a certain amount – usually £50.

The cheque is an order from the client to her bank to pay to

A cheque and cheque guarantee card

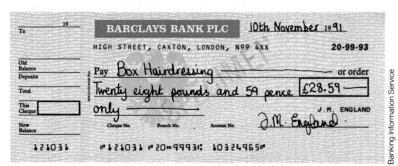

the salon the amount stated, so it needs to be made out correctly. Help your client by making sure the cheque is correct:

1 Check that the cheque is clearly dated, with the date on which you are receiving it.
2 Check that the name of the salon (or person to be paid) is written by the client. If the salon has a stamp for this, offer to print it.
3 Check that the amount to be paid is written both in words and in figures.
4 Check that the cheque has been signed by the client, in your presence.
5 Ask the client for a cheque guarantee card, and write the card number on the back of the cheque. Check that the signature on the card matches the one on the cheque.
6 If the bill is greater than the limit on the cheque guarantee card, ask the client for further identification – such as a driving licence or credit card – so that you can double-check the signature.
7 Write the client's address on the back of the cheque, in case any problems arise later.
8 Check the date of the guarantee card to make sure that the card is valid. If a card is out of date, do not accept the cheque.
9 Place the cheque in the till and return the guarantee card to the client. Give her a receipt.
10 Make sure all cheques are paid into the bank as soon as possible, so that they can be cleared.

Payments by credit card

Some salons have agreements with companies such as Visa and MasterCard so that payments by clients can be made using credit cards. The salon pays a small percentage to credit card companies on all these transactions. It is important that you know which credit cards are accepted by the salon.

If a client wishes to pay by credit card, this is what you do:

1 Check that the card is not out of date. If it is, you cannot accept it.
2 Place the **voucher** and card in the **imprinter** and make sure the card number is transferred clearly to all of the carbon copies.
3 Write details of the services and any purchases on the top copy of the voucher.
4 Write the amount charged.
5 Ask the client to sign the voucher. Check this signature against that on the card.
6 Give the *top* copy to the client as a receipt.
7 Put the other copies in the till and throw away the carbon

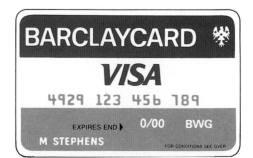

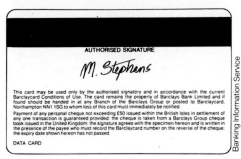

A credit card

Tip

Use a ball-point pen to fill in credit card vouchers, and press quite hard to make sure that what you write is transferred clearly to all the carbon copies.

papers. Copies are kept by the salon – one for the credit card company, the other for salon accounting.

8 Return the card and give the client a receipt.

Other non-cash payments

Charge cards, **account cards** and **gift vouchers** may all be offered in place of cash for payment. Information is freely available from the organisations issuing these. It is important that you know which of these forms of payment are accepted by the salon. Ask a senior member of staff to show you how to deal with these, what forms you need to fill in, and what to do with the vouchers in the till.

Client record systems

An accurate **record system** of all clients ensures that information about hairdressing that has been carried out can be referred to when required. The client's name and telephone number, the stylist's name, the type of perm, the lotion used, the time processed, the results achieved, the date of the last perm, the price charged, and so on, can all be noted down for future use.

A client record card

Model No	Skin Test	Age	Skin Tone	Nat. Colour	Notes		Date first Registered

Hair Condition:		Name:	Address:
Normal ☐	Tex		
Tinted ☐			
Bleach ☐	Style		
Permed ☐			Telephone No.

Date	Remarks	Stylist	Recall Date

Many salons use **record cards**, filed in alphabetical order in a box or cabinet. These cards should be available to all staff at reception. Make sure you understand your salon's record system and know how to fill in and file the record cards correctly. Remember, too, that personal details must always be kept private and confidential.

ACTIVITY

Discuss with your colleagues the requirements for a client record card. Design one that meets these requirements.

Using a computer system

Computers

Computer systems are being used increasingly in salons. Many types are available, and you may be required to operate one. A computer system consists of **hardware** (the equipment) and **software** (the programs), and each computer system has its own special features. In the salon the computer may be used in taking cash and issuing receipts, to total each person's takings, for general accounting, client records, stock records, storing information, and so on. Make sure you understand your salon's system and know how to use it. Remember to ask for help if you run into problems – pressing the wrong button could cause even greater problems!

Hygiene – the science of health

Clients expect the salon to be clean. They expect the towels to have been washed and brushes cleaned. They take it for granted that good **hygiene** is maintained.

You are as responsible as every other member of staff for maintaining the highest standards of cleanliness and hygiene at all times, to safeguard both clients and staff from infection. **Cross-infection** – the passing of disease from one person to another – may follow unhygienic use of washbasins, cups, tools, and so on. If you take sensible precautions the salon can be kept as clean as possible and the risk of cross-infection can be minimised.

☆ Use only clean towels for each customer.
☆ Wash combs and brushes before **sterilising** or **disinfecting** them.
☆ Use 70 per cent alcohol, or alcohol wipes, for cleaning tools.
☆ Keep floors and surfaces clear, tidy and clean.
☆ Maintain good personal and general hygiene – wash your hands regularly, and clean cups and mugs thoroughly.

Many clients are too embarrassed to complain, and are reluctant to do so, when they encounter problems with hygiene or hairdressing service. Ideally the need should not arise, but in case it does, always encourage clients to let the salon know what is wrong so that the problem can be dealt with.

Health and safety

It is when the salon is busiest that the greatest care needs to be taken. Don't let your standards of cleanliness drop, however rushed you may be.

Tip

If clothes are stained, make sure this is noted. Clothes may be returned to the salon for cleaning. Alternatively the client may have this done herself and send the bill for the salon to pay.

Preparing clients

Once a client has arrived for an appointment and you have taken care of her coat and belongings, find out what services have been requested or booked in advance and prepare the client accordingly.

Gowning and protecting

☆ Remember to check that the chair is clean.
☆ Place tissue or a towel over the client's collar and shoulders.
☆ Place a suitably-sized gown in position, and secure it.
☆ If shampooing, place a thicker towel over the shoulders.
☆ If cutting, use cottonwool, tissue or a cutting cape in place of a thicker towel.
☆ If tinting or bleaching, use dark towels, plastic capes, and special tint coverings.
☆ Make sure all clothes are covered and all materials are secured so that they remain in place.
☆ Do not tuck in absorbent materials – they act like sponges. Liquids can seep through and damage clothing.
☆ Make sure nothing falls between the client and the chair back.

Preparing the hair

Hair needs to be free from tangles, hairspray and other materials before it can be worked on. Prepare the client's hair as follows:

1 Loosen the hair by teasing it apart with your fingers.
2 Using a wide-toothed comb or **rake**, start combing the hair points and gradually work upwards to the scalp.
3 Proceed from the neck and sides to the top front.
4 Remove tangles and backcombing without pulling, scratching or breaking the comb.
5 Brush the hair smoothly and firmly, without jerking the client's head.
6 Start brushing at the hair points and gradually work upwards to the scalp.
7 Once the hair is free of tangles, brush in different directions to loosen it.

Combs and combing

Combs come in many shapes and sizes. They may be of vulcanised rubber, tortoise-shell, ivory, wood, metal, bone, horn, or various types of plastic. Some combs are made of synthetic material which cause **static** and make the hair 'flyaway'.

Always use good-quality combs. Badly made combs may break, tearing the hair and scalp. This could result in infection: a broken comb carries germs and is difficult to clean.

Gowning the client

Protecting the client

When using a comb, hold it correctly to avoid straining it or the hair:

☆ hold the comb firmly, with your middle fingers on one side and thumb and little finger on the other;
☆ hold it so that your fingertips cannot slip to the teeth points;
☆ hold it upright – do not flatten or drag it;
☆ use a raking action without tugging;
☆ work from the points to the roots (if you start combing at the roots you will produce more knotting);
☆ support the client's head to prevent discomfort.

Brushes and brushing

Brushes are made from a variety of materials. Good brushes are made from natural **bristles**, such as those of pigs. Others may be wire, plastic or rubber. They are designed for various purposes, such as dressing, or clearing loose hair, so choose the correct type of brush for the job in hand.

For preparing hair, use a firm, tufted brush which takes out tangles. For dressing hair, use a short, tufted brush. Generally, for thick, coarse hair a short natural-bristle or nylon tufted brush is suitable for salon use. For soft, thin hair a longer bristle may be kinder. The brushing action stimulates and distributes natural oil – this is best achieved with a soft, bristle brush. Hair styling requires a variety of brushes, but the personal choice of a brush is finally determined by its weight, length, size and comfort in use.

Brushing should be in a smoothing, stroking action – never harshly scrubbing. Two brushes may be used with a rolling wrist action – one following the other.

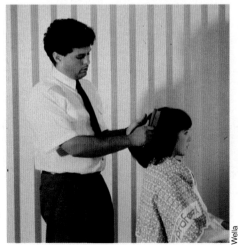
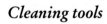

Cleaning tools

☆ Clean tools after use.
☆ Never use tools on another client without cleaning and sterilising them first.
☆ Remove loose material from combs and brushes, wash and disinfect them, then dry them. **Disinfectant cabinets** may be used after drying.
☆ Always rinse liquid disinfectants from tools with plenty of water, otherwise they may irritate the client's skin.

- ☆ Don't leave metal tools too long in liquid disinfectants or disinfecting cabinets, otherwise they will spoil.
- ☆ Always check the manufacturers' instructions before using liquid disinfectants or disinfecting cabinets.

Dealing with complaints

It is not easy to deal with an unsatisfied client – you will need all your skills of tact and diplomacy. Remember that a client has every right to expect the services agreed and paid for. If the salon is at fault, mistakes must be put right.

It can be difficult to decide what is reasonable or unreasonable. Whatever your personal feelings, try to remain calm, polite, and understanding. Arguing back will probably make the client more angry, and is not good for the salon's image. A satisfied client is good business!

If you notice a mistake, don't try to pretend it hasn't happened. Put the situation right before the client leaves the salon. If a client approaches you with a **complaint**, you should:

- ☆ receive the client pleasantly and politely;
- ☆ discuss the nature of the client's complaint;
- ☆ analyse the complaint carefully and sympathetically;
- ☆ diagnose the fault and suggest corrective action;
- ☆ agree with the client what is to be done;
- ☆ carry out the correction then and there, or agree a convenient time for the client to return;
- ☆ for future reference, record the complaint and the action taken.

If the complaint is serious – such as hair breaking off after a perm, or hair becoming discoloured after tinting – there may be difficulties in putting it right. You should then inform your employer who will warn the salon's insurers, as the client has a legal right to claim **compensation**. With tact it may be possible to avoid this by agreeing a course of corrective action and refunding money paid.

Health and safety

Use only good-quality tools which are not likely to damage the hair, and apply them gently and correctly. If you accidentally tear the scalp with a broken brush or comb, report this at once to your tutor or senior. She will clean the wound and then apply a suitable antiseptic to reduce the risk of infection.

ACTIVITY

In threes, use role-play to practise reception duties. One person acts the client, another the receptionist. The third person acts as an observer, noting where the duties are done well, and where things go wrong.

Repeat the activity, with the client complaining about the service received.

Tip

Don't be hurried in trying to put a problem right – you might make a bad situation worse. Always remain calm and give careful consideration to the problem, making sure the client understands and agrees to any course of corrective action.

How to succeed

Checklist

In preparing for assessments on reception, the following list may be useful. Check that you have covered and fully understood these items:

- ☐ showing yourself to be clean, hygienic and efficient;

□ using the telephone effectively;
□ receiving clients pleasantly, politely and courteously;
□ finding out, by questioning and discussion, what services and goods are required;
□ operating the salon's appointment system effectively;
□ preparing clients and their hair;
□ choosing combs and using good combing technique;
□ choosing brushes and using good brushing technique;
□ processing money received for goods and services sold;
□ carefully using and maintaining salon equipment.

Self-check quiz

Oral and written questions are used to test your knowledge and understanding. Try the following:

1 The science of health is called:
   (a) nutrition
   (b) diet
   (c) hygiene
   (d) physiology

2 The following type of brush is the kindest to use:
   (a) nylon
   (b) bristle
   (c) metal
   (d) plastic

3 A suitable comb to use for preparing hair is called:
   (a) a rake comb
   (b) a tailcomb
   (c) a needle comb
   (d) a setting comb

Oral test

With the help of a friend, give spoken answers to the following:

1 What are the advantages of a good comb?
2 How should you receive a client in the salon?
3 Why is it necessary for you to prepare a client for services?
4 Describe the various methods of hair brushing.
5 Describe the correct way to comb long hair.

Written test

Answer the following questions in writing:

1 Imagine that you are preparing a client's hair for services.
   (a) State the types of brushes used.
   (b) Describe brushing techniques.

(c) State the types of combs used.
(d) Describe combing techniques.
(e) Describe methods of cleaning combs and brushes.

2 Suppose that you are receiving a client into the salon.
   (a) Explain the importance of good manners and prompt attention.
   (b) List the receptionist's duties.
   (c) Describe how you find out a client's requirements.
   (d) Describe an appointment system.
   (e) Explain the importance of a client record system.

3 As a receptionist, your work includes administration.
   (a) Why is it important to write down messages you take?
   (b) Why should you always take the caller's name and number?
   (c) Why should calls be kept as brief as possible?
   (d) How, in outline, should you deal with cash?
   (e) Why should you keep a careful note of all monies taken?

Andrew Collinge, for TRESemmé

UNIT 2

Consulting and diagnosing

Professionalism

Each client who walks through the salon door is different, with a unique combination of hair type and colour, skin and scalp condition, past history of hair care, and present requirements. It is your job as a professional to examine the hair and scalp, to assess what state it is in, to ask questions and listen to your client's answers, to decide what treatment is necessary, and to agree with your client on a course of action.

Just as a doctor needs knowledge of medicine and a reassuring bedside manner, so you need knowledge of hair, the scalp and the skin, and the ability to discuss these with your clients clearly, confidently and tactfully. You also need to be able to recognise any problems, and know how to deal with them.

This unit includes detailed information about these aspects of hairdressing. Take time to read it carefully, to learn about the 'raw materials' you will be working with daily.

ACTIVITY

With colleagues, practise asking different types of questions. Ask your tutor to explain the difference between 'open' and 'closed' questions.

The head

The bones

The foundation of the head or skull consists of the bones of the **cranium** (the top, sides, and back of the head) and the bones of the **face**.

☆ The **frontal**, **parietal**, **temporal** and **occipital bones** form the rounded part of the head. This encloses and protects the brain, and the organs of sight and hearing.
☆ The **maxillae**, **mandible**, **malar** and **nasal bones** form the face.
☆ The other bones are inside the skull and form the roof of

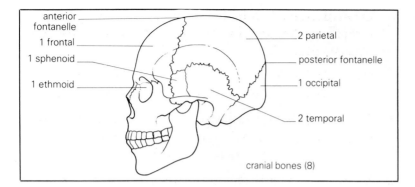

Bones of the cranium

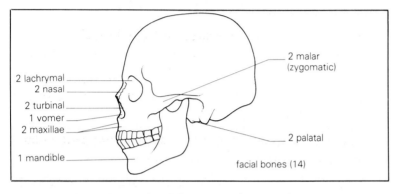

Bones of the face

the mouth, the back of the eye sockets, and structures at the back of the nose.

At birth spaces between the bones of the cranium allow them to glide over each other. The largest spaces between the bones are called **fontanelles**. The two main ones are the **anterior** (front) and **posterior** (back) fontanelles. These are the 'soft spots' on a young baby's head. These soon close together, to form immovable joints called **sutures**.

The muscles

☆ **Occipital-frontalis** A muscle that covers the upper cranium. It connects with the fibrous tendon sheet of the scalp. It lifts the eyebrows, as in frowning, surprise or horror.

ACTIVITY

List the bones of the head. Which of these are important in hair styling?

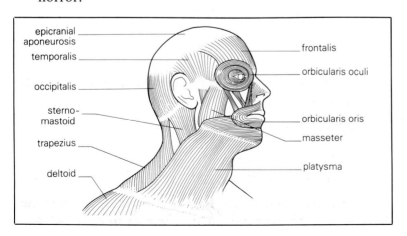

Muscles of the head and face

- ☆ **Orbicularis oculi** Muscles surrounding the eyes. They form the eyelids and close the eyes. They wrinkle the eyes when contracted.
- ☆ **Orbicularis oris** A muscle surrounding the mouth. It forms the lips, closes the mouth, and helps in speaking.
- ☆ **Temporalis** A muscle that connects the temporal bone at the side of the head to the malar arch and the mandible. It closes the mouth and aids in chewing.
- ☆ **Masseter** A muscle situated between the malar arch and mandible. It closes the jaw during chewing.
- ☆ **Zygomaticus** A muscle that runs from the malar to the angle of the mouth. It elevates the lip muscles outwards.
- ☆ **Sternomastoid** A muscle running from the sternum and clavicle to the temporal bone. It flexes the neck, and rotates and bows the head.
- ☆ **Platysma** A muscle within the neck. It wrinkles the skin and depresses the corners of the mouth.
- ☆ **Trapezius** A muscle that forms the upper part of the back, and the sides and back of the neck. It draws the head backwards.

The scalp

The **scalp** is the flexible, protective covering of the top of the head. It consists of the following:

- ☆ **skin**, with hair;
- ☆ **connective tissue**, which firmly attaches the skin to the tendon;
- ☆ the **epicranial aponeurosis**, a sheet of non-elastic fibrous tendon;
- ☆ loose connective tissue between the tendon sheet and the skull bones;
- ☆ the **occipito-frontalis** muscle, which lies between the occipital and frontal bones of the cranium.

The nerves

The main **nerves** concerned with the muscles, skin and glands of the head and neck are as follows:

- ☆ the **5th cranial** nerve (the **trigeminal**);
- ☆ the **7th cranial** nerve (the **facial**);
- ☆ the **11th cranial** nerve (the **spinal accessory**);
- ☆ the **2nd** and **3rd cervical** spinal nerves.

The 5th cranial nerve carries messages to the brain from the facial skin, teeth, nose and mouth. There are three branches:

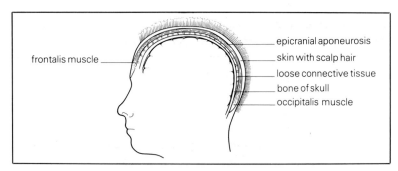

The scalp

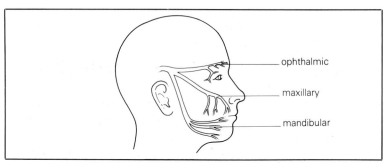

Nerves of the head: 5th cranial (trigeminal) nerve

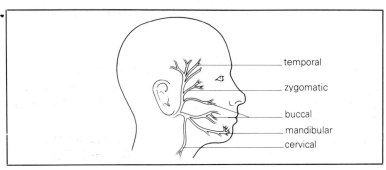

Nerves of the head: 7th cranial (facial) nerve

☆ the **ophthalmic** serves the tear glands, the skin of the forehead, and the upper cheeks;
☆ the **maxillary** serves the upper jaw and the mouth;
☆ the **mandibular** serves the lower jaw muscles, the teeth, and the chewing muscles.

The 7th cranial nerve passes through the temporal bone, behind the ear, and then divides. It serves the ear muscles, the occipitalis, the muscles of facial expression, the tongue and the palate. There are five main branches:

☆ the **temporal**, behind the ear muscles, the orbicularis oculi and the frontalis muscle;
☆ the **zygomatic**, which serves the eye muscles of the orbits;
☆ the **buccal**, which serves the upper lip and the side of the nose;
☆ the **mandibular**, which serves the lower lip, and the mentalis muscle of the chin;
☆ the **cervical**, which serves the platysma muscle of the chin.

The 11th cranial nerve serves the sternomastoid and

trapezius neck muscles, and the deeper structures of the head. It triggers the bending and turning of the head.

The 2nd and 3rd pairs of cervical nerves serve the back of the scalp, the sternomastoid, and the trapezius muscles.

The blood supply

The main blood vessels supplying blood to the head and face are the **carotid arteries**. These sub-divide into the internal and external branches. The internal branch lies deep in the neck and supplies the brain and other parts of the head. The external branch divides into three further main branches:

☆ The **occipital** branch on each side of the head supplies the back and the vertex, of the head and scalp.

☆ The **temporal** branch on each side passes up the side of the face, the side of the head, and the scalp, supplying also the hair follicles and papillae.

☆ The **facial** branch on each side supplies the muscles and tissues of the face. It passes along the chin and up to the front of the head.

Note that **arteries** carry blood *from* the heart.

The blood in the tissues flows through the minute **capillaries**, then into the **venules**, and the larger **veins**. In the head the main veins are the internal and external **jugular veins**. These are situated at the sides of the neck.

The internal jugular vein and its branch, the **facial vein**, carry blood from the face and deep within the head. The external jugular vein carries blood from the scalp, hair follicles and papillae. It has two branches: the **occipital** and the

Blood supply to the head

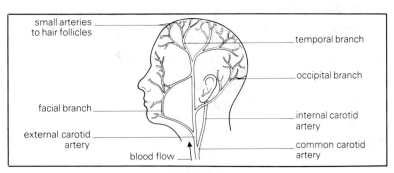

Blood supply from the head

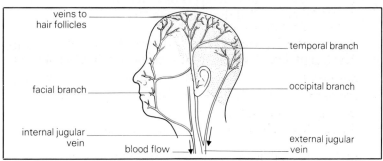

temporal. These carry blood from those areas supplied by the carotid artery branches. The jugular veins join with the **subclavian veins**, which lie about an inch above the clavicle.

Note that **veins** carry blood *to* the heart.

The skin

The **skin** is the outer covering of the body. It is a complex and important organ, made up of different layers and containing many parts: oil and sweat glands, hair muscles, blood and lymph vessels, nerves and sensory organs.

The skin has four main functions: protection, temperature control, secretion and excretion, and sensation.

☆ **Protection** The skin forms a tough, flexible, physical barrier. It keeps excess water out, and body fluids in. The oil and sweat it produces are acid, helping to prevent bacterial growth. Melanin pigment in skin helps to filter out harmful rays of the sun. Vitamin D is produced in the skin, in the presence of sunlight, which helps to maintain body health.

☆ **Temperature control** The hair, hair muscles, and sweat glands help to maintain the normal body temperature of 37 °C. In cold weather, muscles make the hairs stand up, trapping an insulating layer of warm air over the surface of the skin. In hot weather the sweat glands excrete water which evaporates from the skin, cooling the body.

☆ **Secretion and excretion** Oil or sebum is used as a protective covering, waterproofing and lubricating the skin and hair. Waste products such as **urea** are passed out of the body via sweat.

☆ **Sensation** Beneath the top layer of the skin are nerves and sense organs. The many nerve endings are responsible for feelings of heat, cold, pain and touch. These sensations protect the body from harm.

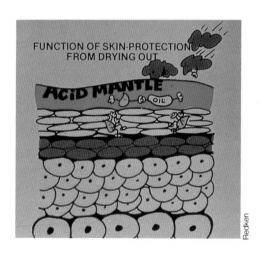

The epidermis

The skin consists of several layers of different cell tissue. The outermost layer is called the **epidermis**. It has five distinct layers:

☆ The **horny layer** is the hard, cornified top layer of skin. It is constantly being worn away and replaced by underlying tissue.

☆ The **clear layer** is transparent and colourless, allowing colour from below to be seen. There is no melanin, but the cells contain keratin.

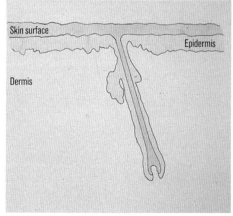

☆ The **granular layer** lies between the softer living cells below and the hardened dead cells above. It contains granular tissues.

☆ The **mixed layer** consists of mixed cells. Immediately below the granular layer lie **prickle cells** (spiny cells) which are softer, alive and active. Below these lie the **Malpighian cells**, which contain **melanin**, the skin colour pigment. (The names **stratum aculeatum**, **stratum spinosum** and **stratum Malpighi** are also used for this mixed layer of cells.)

☆ The **germinating layer** is the lowest or base layer of the epidermis. It is the site of most active growth. The cells are softer and fuller than those above. The germinating layer connects with the underlying dermis.

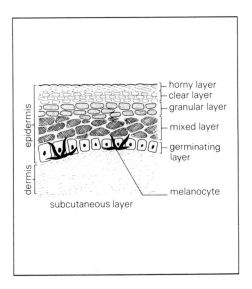

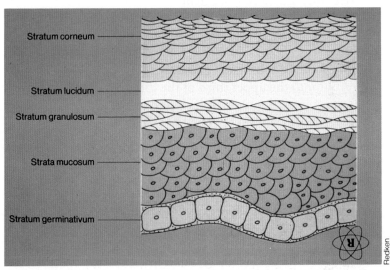

The skin (*left*); layers of the epidermis (*right*)

The dermis

The **dermis** is the largest layer of the skin. It is here that the hair follicle is formed. The dermis is made up of elastic and connective tissue, and is well supplied with blood and lymph vessels. The skin receives its nutrient supply from this area. The upper part of the dermis, the **papillary layer**, contains the organs of touch, heat and cold, and pain. The lower part of the dermis, the **reticular layer**, forms a looser network of cells.

The subcutaneous tissue

The **subcutaneous tissue** lies below the dermis. It is also known as the **subcutis**, or occasionally as the **hypodermis**. It is composed of loose cell tissue and contains stores of fat. The base of the hair follicle is situated just above this area, or sometimes in it. Subcutaneous tissue gives roundness to the body and fills the space between the dermis and muscle tissue that may lie below.

The hair follicle

Hair grows from a thin, tubelike, space in the skin called a **hair follicle**.

☆ At the bottom of the follicles are areas well supplied with nerves and blood vessels, which nourish the cellular activity. These are called **hair papillae**.

☆ Immediately surrounding each papilla is the **germinal matrix** which consists of actively forming hair cells.

☆ As the new hair cells develop the lowest part of the hair is shaped into the **hair bulb**.

☆ The cells continue to shape the form as they push along the follicle until they appear at the skin surface as **hair fibres**.

☆ The cells gradually harden and die. The hair is formed of dead tissue. It retains its elasticity due to its chemical structure and keratin content.

Oil

The oil gland, or **sebaceous gland**, is situated in the skin and opens out into the upper third of the follicle. From it **oil**, or **sebum**, is secreted into the follicle and onto the hair and skin surface. Sebum helps to prevent the skin and hair from drying. By retaining moisture it helps the hair and skin to stay pliable. Sebum is slightly acid – about pH 5.6 – and forms a protective anti-bacterial covering for the skin.

Sweat

The **sweat glands**, or **sudoriferous glands**, lie adjacent to the hair follicle and are appendages of the skin. They secrete sweat which passes out through the sweat ducts. The ends of these ducts can be seen at the surface of the skin as sweat **pores**.

There are two types of sweat gland: the larger, associated closely with hair follicles, are the **apocrine glands**; the smaller, found over most of the skin's surface, are the **eccrine glands**.

Sweat is mainly water with salt, and other minerals may be present. In abnormal conditions sweat contains larger amounts of waste material. Evaporation of sweat cools the skin. The function of sweat, and thus the sweat glands, is to protect the body by helping to maintain the normal temperature.

The hair muscle

The **hair muscle**, or **arrector pili**, is attached at one end to the hair follicle, and at the other to the underlying tissue of the epidermis. When it contracts it pulls the hair and follicle upright. Upright hairs trap a warm layer of air around the skin. The hairs also act as a warning system – for example, you are quickly aware of an insect crawling over your skin!

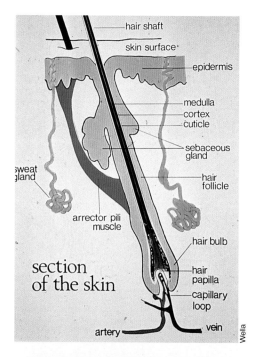

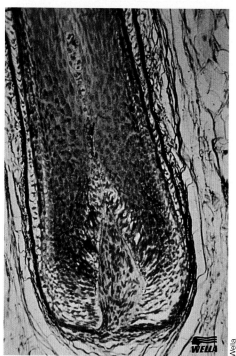

The hair papilla and germinal matrix

ACTIVITY

Draw an outline of a hair, in its follicle, in the skin. Label the different parts.

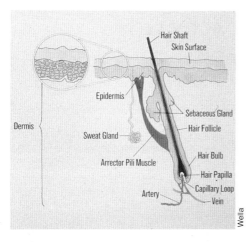

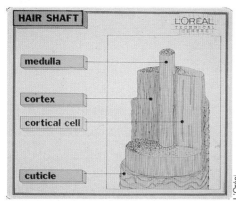

The hair

Many hairdressing processes depend on certain properties of hair. This section introduces you to the structure and chemistry of hair.

The structure of hair

Hairs are fine strands of tissue which appear above the skin surface. They cover most of the body, with the exception of the eyelids, the palms of the hands and the soles of the feet. There are three different types of hair:

☆ **Lanugo hair** Fine, downy hair that covers the body of the unborn child: it is lost just before or around birth.

☆ **Vellus hair** Fine, short, fluffy hair which covers most parts of the body. It can be seen clearly on the faces of women.

☆ **Terminal hair** Longer, coarser hair, found on the head, on the faces of men, in ears and eyebrows, on the arms, legs and chest, and in the pubic region.

Each hair has the same basic structure. There are three layers:

☆ **Cuticle** The outer layer of colourless cells, which forms a protective surface to the hair. It regulates the chemicals entering and damaging the hair, and protects the hair from excessive heat and drying. The cells overlap, like rooftiles: if you rub a hair from base to tip it feels smooth, but if you rub it from tip to base it feels rough.

☆ **Cortex** The middle and largest layer, consisting of long spiral chains of cells like springs. Each cell is made of bundles of fibres. The way these fibres and cells are held together determines the strength of hair, its thickness, curl and elasticity. **Pigments** in the cortex give hair its natural colour.

☆ **Medulla** The central space of the hair. It serves no useful purpose, and is not always present.

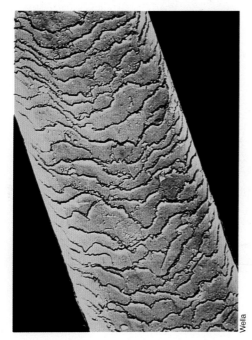

The hair cuticle

Chemical properties of hair

The bundles of fibres found in the cortex are made from even smaller components, as the diagram shows. **Amino acids** are molecules which contain atoms of different chemical **elements**. There are about twenty-two amino acids in hair, and the relative proportions of elements are different in each. Overall, the elements in hair are in approximately these proportions:

carbon   50%
oxygen   21%
nitrogen   18%
hydrogen   7%
sulphur   4%

The amino acids are combined to form larger molecules, long **polypeptide chains** called **proteins**. One of the most important of these is **keratin**. Keratin is an important component of nails, skin and hair: it is this protein that makes them flexible and **elastic**. Because of the keratin it contains, hair can be stretched and compressed, curled and waved.

ACTIVITY

List the functions of the hair and skin. How may these be affected by hairdressing processes, both physical and chemical?

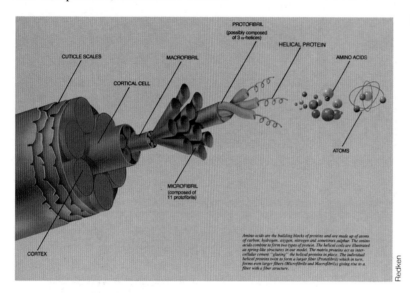

Inside the hair

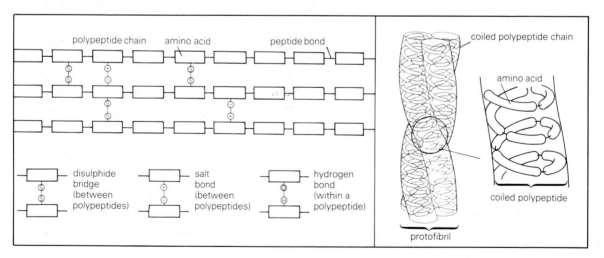

Cross-links within hair

In hair, keratin forms long chains which coil up like springs. They are held in this shape by cross-links between chains. The three kinds of link are **disulphide bonds (sulphur bonds)**, **salt bonds**, and **hydrogen bonds**. Salt bonds and hydrogen bonds are relatively weak and can be broken, allowing the springs to be stretched out: this is what happens in curling. The normal, coiled form of keratin is called **alpha-keratin**; when it has been stretched, set and dried it is called **beta-keratin**. The change is only temporary: once the hair has been made wet, or has gradually absorbed moisture from the air, it relaxes back to the alpha state. Disulphide bonds are much stronger, but these too can be altered, as in perming.

Hair in its 'alpha' and 'beta' forms, before and after curling

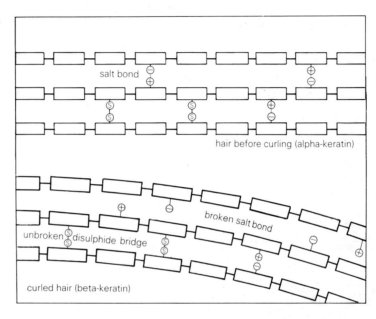

ACTIVITY

Examine a colleague's hair and scalp. Note the condition of the hair and the skin, the hair length and its colour, and whether the hair has been permed, tinted, etc.

Physical properties of hair

Hair naturally contains a certain amount of water, which lubricates it, allowing it to stretch and re-coil. Hair that is dry and in poor condition is less elastic.

Hair is **hygroscopic**: it absorbs water from the surrounding air. How much water is taken up depends on the dryness of the hair and the moistness of the atmosphere. Hair is also **porous**: there are tiny tube-like spaces within the hair structure, and the water flows into these by **capillary action**, rather as blotting paper absorbs ink. Drying hair in the ordinary way evaporates only the surface moisture, but drying over long periods or at abnormally high temperatures removes water from *within* the hair, leaving it brittle and in poor condition. Damaged hair is less porous than healthy hair, and easily loses any water: this makes it hard to stretch and mould.

Hair porosity

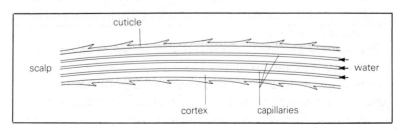

Curled hair returns to its former shape as it takes up water, so the drier the atmosphere, the longer the curl or set lasts. Similarly, curling dry hair is most effective just after the hair has been washed, because although the surface is dry the hair will have absorbed water internally. Blow-styling and curling with hot irons, heated rollers, hot combs and hot brushes all have similar temporary effects.

Hair growth

Hair is constantly growing. Over a period of one to six years an individual hair actively grows, then stops, rests and degenerates, and finally falls out. Before the hair leaves the follicle the new hair is normally ready to replace it. If a hair is not replaced then a tiny area of baldness results.

The lives of individual hairs vary and are subject to variations in the body. Some are actively growing while others are resting. Hairs on the head are at different stages of growth.

Stages of growth

The life cycle of hair is as follows:

☆ **Anagen** The active growing stage of the hair, a period of activity of the papilla and germinal matrix. This stage may last from a few months to several years. It is at this stage of formation at the base of the follicle that the hair's thickness, shape, and texture is determined. Hair colour, too, is formed in the early part of anagen.

☆ **Catagen** A period when the hair stops growing but cellular activity continues at the papilla. The hair bulb gradually separates from the papilla and moves further up the follicle.

☆ **Telogen** The final stage, when there is no further growth or activity at the papilla. The follicle begins to shrink, and completely separates from the papilla area. This resting stage does not last long: towards the end of the telogen stage, cells begin to activate in preparation for the new anagen stage of regrowth.

The new anagen period involves the hair follicle beginning to grow down again. Vigorous papilla activity generates a new hair at the germinal matrix. At the same time the old hair is slowing making its way up and out of the follicle. Often the old and new hair can be seen at the same time in the follicle.

In some animals hair development occurs at an even pace, resulting in moulting. Human hair, however, develops at an uneven rate and few follicles are shedding their hair at the same time. (If all hairs fell at the same time we would have bald periods!)

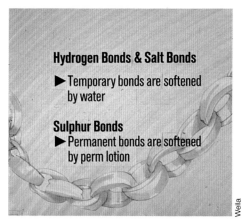

Hydrogen Bonds & Salt Bonds
▶ Temporary bonds are softened by water

Sulphur Bonds
▶ Permanent bonds are softened by perm lotion

Chemical bonds in hair

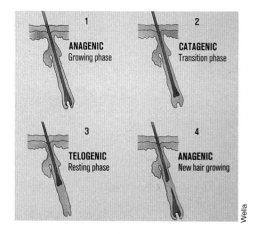

The life cycle of hair

Regeneration of the hair

The regeneration of hair is influenced by the following factors:

- ☆ health;
- ☆ diet;
- ☆ age;
- ☆ sex;
- ☆ hormone balance;
- ☆ heredity factors;
- ☆ climate;
- ☆ physical conditions;
- ☆ chemical effects;
- ☆ effects of disease.

Human hair is grouped into the following types:

- ☆ **Caucasian** (European) Loosely waved or straight hair.

- ☆ **Negroid** (African) Tight, kinked, woolly, curled hair.

- ☆ **Mongoloid** (Asian) Coarse, straight, lank hair.

The differences between these groups are distinctive, and form an interesting study for forensic scientists.

Hair types

Hair colour

The **natural colour** of hair depends on the amounts and proportions of **pigment** it contains. Two types of pigment are found in hair: melanin and pheomelanin.

- ☆ **Melanin** gives black and brown colours. Dark ash-brown hair contains a lot of melanin.

- ☆ **Pheomelanin** gives red and yellow colours. Blonde hair contains relatively little melanin.

White and albino hair contains little or no pigment.

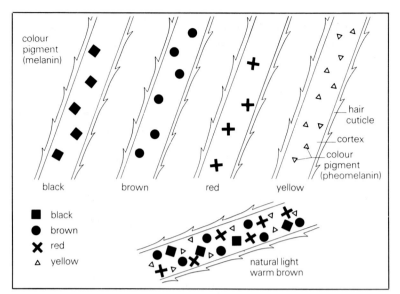

Neutralising, tinting and bleaching are chemical processes, called **oxidation reactions**, which act on these pigments to change the hair colour.

Diseases, hair defects and hygiene

Diseases

Inside us, and on our skin and hair, we all carry large numbers of **micro-organisms**. These are very small organisms such as **bacteria**, **fungi** and **viruses**. Individual cells are so small that they cannot be seen with the naked eye: bacteria and fungi can be seen through a microscope, but viruses are too small even for that. However, we may be able to see large numbers, or **colonies**, of bacteria or fungi.

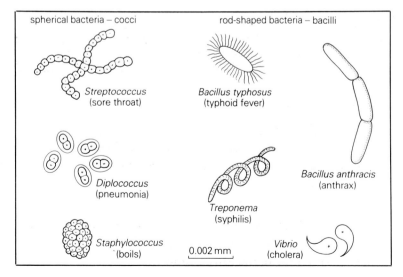

ACTIVITY

Arrange with your tutors a visit to the library or a biology laboratory at your local college. Look at a range of pictures to help you recognise different hair and scalp diseases. Make notes of what you see.

Alternatively, you might be able to visit your local hospital or clinic and get first-hand information about consultation and diagnosis.

Many micro-organisms are quite harmless, but some can cause diseases: these are called **pathogens** (or **germs**). Flu, for example, is caused by a virus, thrush by a fungus, and bronchitis often by bacteria. Those germs that can be transmitted from one person to another are said to be **infectious**. The body is naturally resistant to infection: it fights pathogens using the **immune system**. So we may carry pathogenic organisms without necessarily having any disease. And there are many diseases that aren't caused by micro-organisms.

The skin may also provide a home for tiny **insects** such as lice, and these too can cause disease.

Treatment

When you have a disease, the **symptoms** are the visible signs that something is wrong: they are produced by the infection and by the reactions of the body. Symptoms help you to recognise the disease.

Infectious diseases should always be treated by a general practitioner. Non-infectious conditions and defects can often be treated in the salon or with products available from chemists, or by a specialist such as a **trichologist**.

Hygiene

A warm, humid salon can be a perfect home for germs. Given nourishment in the form of dirt and dust, they may reproduce rapidly. This is why it is important to keep the salon clean at all times, including clothing, work surfaces, tools and other equipment. A tidy salon is easier to clean, so get into the habit of clearing up as you work.

Health and safety

Find out more about hair and scalp diseases and defects. There are other textbooks that give more details. When examining clients, make your observations carefully. Check your diagnosis with a tutor or senior.

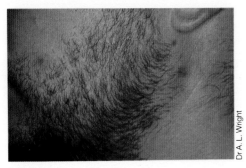

Sycosis

Dr A. L. Wright

Bacterial infectious diseases

☆ **Furunculosis** Boils and abcesses.
Cause A staphylococcal infection of hair follicles.
Symptoms Raised, inflamed, pus-filled spots; there is irritation, swelling and pain.
Treatment By a doctor.

☆ **Sycosis** A bacterial infection of the hairy parts of the face.
Cause Bacteria attack the upper part of the hair follicle; this may spread to the lower follicle.

Symptoms Small, yellow spots around the follicle mouth; burning, irritation, and general inflammation.
Treatment Antibiotics, given by a doctor.

☆ **Impetigo** A bacterial infection of the upper layers of the skin.
Cause A staphylococcal or streptococcal infection.
Symptoms First, a burning sensation; spots appear and become dry; honey-coloured crusts form; spots merge to form larger areas.
Treatment Antibiotics, given by a doctor.

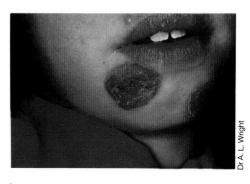

Impetigo

☆ **Folliculitis** Inflammation of the hair follicles.
Cause A bacterial infection; or chemical or physical actions.
Symptoms Inflamed follicles. These are a common symptom of certain skin diseases.
Treatment By a doctor.

Viral infectious diseases

☆ **Herpes simplex (cold sore)** A viral infection of the skin.
Cause Possibly exposure to extreme heat or cold, or reaction to food or drugs; skin may carry the virus for many years.
Symptoms Burning, irritation, swelling and inflammation precedes the appearance of fluid-filled blisters; these are common on the lips and the surrounding tissues.
Treatment By a doctor.

☆ **Herpes zoster (shingles)** A viral infection of the epidermis and nerve endings.
Cause Perhaps from chickenpox in earlier years, which may have lain dormant in the skin before erupting.
Symptoms Painful blisters appear, often on one side only, of the head or body: sore, inflamed areas result. This may be preceded by a fever. Aching and pain may continue after the condition has cleared.
Treatment By a doctor.

☆ **Influenza (common cold)** Viral infections of the body.
Cause Viruses, which attack cells of the body.
Symptoms High temperatures, fever, sneezing, aching, etc.
Treatment By a doctor, if serious; or with cold-relief treatments from a chemist.

☆ **Warts (verrucae)** A viral infection of the skin.
Cause The lower epidermis is attacked by the virus, which causes the skin to harden and the skin cells to multiply.
Symptoms Raised, roughened skin, often brown or discoloured. There may be irritation and soreness. Warts are common on exposed areas such as the hands or face.
Treatment By a doctor.

Fungal infectious diseases

☆ **Tinea capitis** Ringworm of the head.
Cause Fungal infection of the skin or hair.
Symptoms Circular areas of grey or white skin, surrounded by red, active rings; hairs broken close to the skin, which looks dull and rough. It is common in children.
Treatment By a doctor.

☆ **Tinea pedis (athlete's foot)** Ringworm of the feet.
Cause A fungus attacks the skin between the toes, which becomes soft and soggy. The disease is common to those using swimming pools and not drying their feet thoroughly, and those standing for long periods (including hairdressers).
Symptoms Soft, sore skin; sometimes bleeding; a bad odour; some irritation.
Treatment By a doctor, or by products from a chemist.

Diseases caused by animal parasites

☆ **Scabies** An allergic skin reaction to the itch mite.
Cause A tiny animal mite, *Sarcoptes scabiei*, which burrows through the skin, where it lays its eggs.
Symptoms A rash in the skin folds, around the midriff and on the insides of the thighs. It becomes extremely itchy at night. There are reddish spots and burrows (greyish lines) under the skin. Scabies is not found on the head or scalp except in children under 2 years.
Treatment By a doctor.

☆ **Pediculosis capitis** Infestation of the head by lice.
Cause Pediculus humanus capitis, the head louse, attacks the skin and feeds by puncturing the skin to suck the blood; it lays eggs (**ova**) on the hair, close to the skin.
Symptoms An itchy reaction like a mosquito bite. Some people develop an allergic reaction, with itchy red marks. Lice can be seen by parting the hair; more commonly the eggs or hatched eggs (**nits**) can be seen stuck to the hairs. Live eggs are found close to the scalp. Lice are passed only by actual contact between an infected head and another head.
Treatment By a doctor, or by products from a chemist.

Non-infectious conditions of skin and hair

☆ **Acne** A disorder of the hair follicles and sebaceous glands.
Cause This is not fully understood, but increased sebum and other matter blocks the follicle: the skin reacts to this blockage as though it were a foreign body such as a splinter.

The head louse

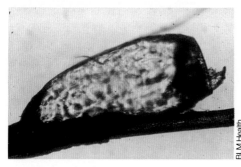

A nit, or hatched egg

Symptoms Raised spots or bumps in the skin, commonly on the face and forehead; soreness, irritation, and inflammation; severe cases produce cysts and scarring.
Treatment By a doctor.

☆ **Alopecia** Baldness or thinning of hair. **Alopecia areata** is the name given to baldness in circular areas; it is common on the scalp. If the condition continues, these areas join to form **alopecia totalis**, complete hair loss from the scalp. **Alopecia universalis** is complete baldness of the body.
Causes The hair follicles are unable to produce new hairs to replace the old ones. **Male-pattern alopecia** is baldness found in the teenage years of men and the later years of women; its cause is hereditary, and treatment can be given by the salon, a trichologist or a doctor. **Cicatrical alopecia** is baldness due to scarring of the skin arising from chemical or physical injury. The hair follicles are damaged and permanent baldness results.
Symptoms Areas of thinning or diffuse hair; in alopecia areata there are small hairs in a pale pink smooth area. These hairs are thinner near the scalp.
Treatment By a doctor or a trichologist.

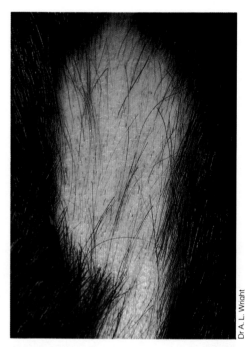

Alopecia areata

Dr A. L. Wright

☆ **Canities** Grey or white hair.
Cause Colour pigment not forming in the new hair.
Symptoms The presence of white hairs.
Treatment Tinting.

☆ **Eczema; dermatitis** At its simplest, red, inflamed skin.
Causes There are several, with either internal or external factors: it may be due to physical irritation or to an allergic response.
Symptoms These range from slightly inflamed areas of skin, to severe splitting and weeping areas; there may be irritation, soreness and pain; in advanced states the skin may become infected.
Treatment By a doctor.

☆ **Dandruff (pityriasis capitis)** Dry, scaling scalp.
Cause Fungal infection, or physical or chemical irritants.
Symptoms Dry, small, irritating flakes (or scales) of skin; if the scale becomes moist and greasy it sticks to the skin and the condition known as **scurf** results. Dandruff can be accompanied by **conjunctivitis** (inflammation of the eye) or **blepharitis** (inflammation of the eyelid).
Treatment By various anti-dandruff medicines and shampoos.

☆ **Seborrhoea** Excessive greasiness of the skin and hair.
Cause Over-production of sebum, which may be due to physical or chemical irritants.
Symptoms Very greasy, lank hair, and greasy skin, which makes grooming and dressing of the hair difficult.

Treatment Regular washing, with a minimum of physical or chemical stimulation; in extreme cases it is best treated by a trichologist or a doctor.

☆ **Psoriasis** An inflamed, abnormal thickening of the skin.
Cause Unknown.
Symptoms Areas of thickened skin, which may be raised and circular; silvery or yellow scales may be present; the skin may be sore, itchy, or painful.
Treatment By a doctor or a dermatologist.

Defects of the hair

☆ **Fragilitas crinium (split ends)** Fragile, poorly conditioned hair.
Cause Harsh physical or chemical treatments.
Symptoms Dry, splitting hair-ends.
Treatment Cutting hair-ends and using conditioners.

Fragilitas crinium

☆ **Monilethrix** Beaded hair.
Cause Irregular development of the hair when forming in the follicle.
Symptoms Beadlike swellings and constrictions of the hair shafts; hair often breaks close to the skin.
Treatment By a doctor; conditioning may help.

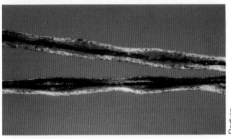
Monilethrix

☆ **Ringed hair** Alternating white and coloured rings of the hair shaft.
Cause Irregular distribution of pigment during hair formation or regeneration.
Symptoms Distinct bands of coloured and colourless hair – there may be few or many.
Treatment There are few effective treatments other than hair colouring.

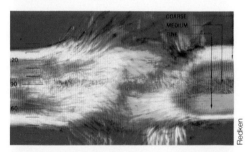
Trichorrhexis nodosa

☆ **Trichorrhexis nodosa** Nodules on the hair shaft, containing splitting sections of hair.
Cause Harsh physical or chemical treatments.
Symptoms Areas of swelling nodules and lengthwise splitting of the hair.
Treatment Cutting at the ends may help, as may conditioning with hair thickeners, etc.

☆ **Sebaceous cyst** Swellings of sebaceous or oil glands.
Cause The sebaceous gland becomes blocked, possibly due to growth of cells arising from the gland wall.
Symptoms Bumps, lumps or swellings, 12–50 mm across, on the scalp, soft to the touch owing to fluid content.
Treatment Removal of the contents, by a doctor.

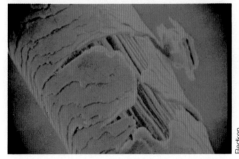
A damaged hair cuticle

☆ **Damaged cuticle** Broken, split, torn hair.
Cause Harsh physical or chemical treatments.
Symptoms Rough, raised, missing areas of cuticle; hair

loses its moisture and becomes dry and porous.
Treatment By conditioners, thickeners, restructurants, etc.

Hair conditions and defects

Diseases are not the only kinds of disorder you will meet. There are various **conditions** of hair that are caused by reactions to physical and chemical processes like backcombing and bleaching. These are non-infectious: they cannot be passed to another person.

There are also **defects**, caused by irregular hair growth. Some are hereditary, and may be shared by members of the same family; others are due, for example, to the abnormal structure of hair follicles. Damage caused by harsh treatment can lead to hair defects.

Damaged hair

Health risks

You need to be able to recognise skin and hair diseases, and be hygienic in your work. This will help you to avoid catching diseases yourself, or passing them from one client to another.

Two other health risks are also important to hairdressers: you should know about these as well.

AIDS

The **acquired immune-deficiency syndrome (AIDS)** is not itself a disease – it's a condition that makes the body *vulnerable* to diseases. It is these other diseases that may actually lead to death. Because AIDS is often fatal and because there is as yet no known cure, it may seem very frightening. Nevertheless, some fears about AIDS result simply from misunderstanding. To protect yourself and your clients, you need to understand the condition.

AIDS is caused by a virus known as the **human immunodeficiency virus (HIV)**. This virus attacks the body's immune system and may make it less effective, leaving the body vulnerable to other infections. But some people carry the HIV virus – they are **HIV-positive** – *without* having AIDS. Anyone who is HIV-positive is potentially able to pass the virus to someone else.

You can become infected only if your body fluids, such as your blood, come into contact with body fluids of someone who is HIV-positive. This most commonly occurs during unprotected sex: condoms help to protect both partners. But this is not the only way – drug addicts who share needles are at risk, and the virus can be transferred through a cut or through broken skin. Remember that infection only occurs through the exchange of body fluids. The virus is sensitive to its

ACTIVITY

Some people are unnecessarily frightened about AIDS, others take unnecessary risks. Find out more about this condition. Discuss your feelings about it, and how it should affect your work.

surroundings, and cannot live long outside the body – so you can't catch it from a toilet seat, for example. Blood for transfusions is now specially checked to make sure that it does not contain HIV.

Hepatitis B

This infection of the liver is another disease caused by a virus. The **hepatitis B virus** (**HBV**) is transmitted through infected blood, body tissue fluids and infected water.

The disease is long-lasting and weakening, and can be fatal. Successful treatments are available, but the virus is very resistant and is said to last a long time outside the human body. Good hygiene is therefore essential. Disinfection, sterilisation and the use of detergents and bleach for washing surfaces is thought to help.

Inoculation is available to protect against HBV. It should be seriously considered by all those who may be at risk, including hairdressers, beauty therapists, electrolysists and manicurists.

Hygiene

In the salon, so long as you take sensible precautions there should be no risk to you or your clients. It is essential that you are thorough in sterilising all equipment, particularly that used for electrolysis, ear piercing and tattooing. Good hygiene, correct disinfection, and protection of any cut or open skin will reduce the dangers not just of HIV/AIDS and hepatitis B but of all diseases.

☆ Keep any cuts and open skin wounds covered.
☆ Wash your hands regularly.
☆ Clear away spilt blood from all surfaces, applying bleach, detergents or disinfectants. Wear rubber gloves.
☆ Do not use tools on clients without first cleaning and sterilising the tools.
☆ Use only sterile, disposable razors or needles on, or in, the skin.
☆ Wrap any blood-soaked materials carefully and place them in a special covered bin.
☆ Arrange removal and disposal of suspect materials by the Local Health Authority.

Consulting and diagnosing technique

Consultation is the process of giving and receiving information. You, as the professional, already know a lot about hair in general, but your client is more familiar than you are with her own hair and how it behaves. Listen to what she tells you; find out what she wants, and examine the hair to see whether there are any factors which limit the treatment you can give. Then at the end of the consultation you will be ready to give appropriate advice.

Examining the hair

Here are some of the questions you can ask yourself:

☆ Is the hair dry, brittle, or breaking?
☆ Is it extremely greasy?
☆ Is the hair too short or uneven?
☆ Is there too much frizz or perm from previous treatment?
☆ Is there variation in synthetic colouring?
☆ What have been the effects of physical processes, e.g. crimping or tonging?
☆ What have been the effects of chemical processes, e.g. perming or colouring?
☆ Have incompatible chemicals been used, such as home hair treatments that leave metallic salts which might react with hydrogen peroxide during bleaching?

Diagnosis like this may tell you whether hair will stand up to processes such as perming. (Further aspects of hair, such as hair growth patterns, are considered in Unit 5.)

You should also be able now to recognise infections and diseases of the hair and scalp. It's important to avoid **cross-infection** – carrying an infection from one person to another – so remember these points:

☆ Make sure you are free of infection yourself, and that your hands are clean.
☆ Examine the hair and scalp before any hairdressing treatment. Divide the hair so that you can see the scalp. Feel the hair for roughness. Smell the hair to detect chemicals.
☆ If you find signs of disease or infection, do not carry out any hairdressing but ask a senior hairdresser to give a second opinion. If she agrees with you, the senior will then tell the client tactfully, and suggest a visit to the doctor as soon as possible.
☆ If you notice the infection when you have already started hairdressing, finish what you are doing and then consult with a senior. Allow the client to leave as soon as possible, without coming into contact with others.
☆ Sterilise all equipment and disinfect the area where you were working.
☆ Stay quiet and unflustered, so as not to cause anxiety to other clients.

ACTIVITY
Bleach some samples of hair to varying degrees of lightness. Rinse, clear, and dry them. Then wind and perm them all, using the same size of curlers, the same length of time (5 or 10 minutes), and the same perm lotions. Compare the results.

ACTIVITY
With a colleague, take turns at being the client or hairdresser in the consultation process. Notice the kinds of remark or question that gain most information, and note how one question may lead to another.

ACTIVITY

Collect samples of hair from your salon – these can be used for various hair-testing procedures. Longer pieces will be more useful, but lengths of 5 cm or more can be used. Collect and store the hair carefully, preferably in envelopes.

ACTIVITY

Carry out each of the tests listed in this unit. Take careful notes of each result. Make sure that you list exactly what is done, the time taken, and the materials used. Use part of the hair sample as a 'before' example, to be compared with the 'after' result. Keep these carefully in your notebook or folder.

Testing the hair and skin

There are various tests you can make to help diagnose the condition of your client's hair. These tests will help you decide what actions to take before applying hairdressing processes. Results of tests should be noted on the client's record card. Skin allergies are considered in Unit 9.

- ☆ **Skin test** (also known as the **pre-disposition test, patch test** or **Sabouraud–Rousseau test**) A test to assess the reaction of the skin to a chemical product. It is used particularly before tinting (see Unit 9).

- ☆ **Strand test** A test used to assess the resultant colour on a strand or section of hair while colour is processing and developing (see Unit 9).

- ☆ **Test cutting** A test in which a piece of hair cut from the head is processed to check its suitability, the amount of processing required and the timing, before the process is carried out. This test is used for colouring, straightening, reducing synthetic colouring, bleaching and incompatibility (see Unit 9).

- ☆ **Test curl** A test made on the hair to determine the lotion suitability, the strength, the curler size, the timing of processing and the development. It is used before perming (see Unit 8).

- ☆ **Curl check or test** A test used to assess development of curl in the perming process. This test is used periodically throughout a perm and for final assessment (see Unit 8).

- ☆ **'Peroxide' test** A test made on hair that has been stripped of its synthetic colour. This test is used to assess the effectiveness of the process (see Unit 9).

- ☆ **Incompatibility test** A test to detect chemicals already on the hair which could react adversely with the chemicals used in hairdressing processes such as colouring and perming (see Units 8 and 9).

- ☆ **Elasticity test** A test to determine how much the hair will stretch and then return to its original position. By taking a hair or hairs between the fingers and extending it or them, you can assess the amount of spring or elasticity. If the hair breaks easily then further tests are required, e.g. a test curl (see Unit 8).

- ☆ **Porosity test** A test to assess the ability of the hair to absorb moisture or liquids. If the cuticle is torn or broken then absorption may be quick. If the cuticle is smooth, unbroken, and tightly packed, it may resist the passage of moisture or liquids. By running the fingertips through the hair, from points to roots, you can assess the degree of roughness (see Unit 8).

How to succeed

Checklist

In preparing for assessments on consulting and diagnosing, the following list may be helpful. Check that you have covered and fully understood these items:

- [ ] recognising differences between good and poor hair;
- [ ] considering effects of chemicals on virgin and treated hair;
- [ ] differentiating between diseases, conditions and defects of hair and scalp;
- [ ] taking precautions to prevent cross-infection;
- [ ] using a variety of tests to analyse conditions of hair;
- [ ] determining actions to improve hair and scalp states;
- [ ] displaying tact, understanding and interpersonal skills;
- [ ] determining hair growth patterns and problems that must be overcome;
- [ ] identifying different parts of the hair and skin;
- [ ] recognising different applications of perm, tint, etc.;
- [ ] dealing with differences between clients' requirements and test results on their hair or skin;
- [ ] identifying advice and guidance required by clients;
- [ ] explaining the effects of hairdressing services, materials and products.

Self-check quiz

Oral and written questions are used to test your knowledge and understanding. Try the following:

1 Hair grows from:
   (a) the cortex
   (b) the root
   (c) the papilla
   (d) the epidermis

2 The epicranial aponeurosis is:
   (a) a muscle
   (b) a bone
   (c) part of the skin
   (d) part of the scalp

3 Alopecia is:
   (a) an infection
   (b) non-infectious
   (c) caused by a pathogen
   (d) caused by a bacterium

Oral test

With the help of a friend, give spoken answers to the following:

1 Name the layers of the skin.
2 Name the parts of the hair follicle from which the hair grows.
3 State precautions to be taken with hair that has been chemically treated before.
4 Name two bacterially-caused diseases, and describe their symptoms.
5 Outline tests that may be used on hair and skin.
6 What are the differences between diseases, conditions and defects?
7 What is cross-infection?

Written test

Answer the following questions in writing:

1 Describe the hair and follicle:
   (a) name the different parts;
   (b) list the functions;
   (c) describe hair growth and replacement;
   (d) describe natural hair colour;
   (e) state the different ethnic hair groups.

2 Imagine that you are dealing with hair of poor condition.
   (a) What precautions should you take in applying different processes?
   (b) What conditioning treatments could you use?
   (c) Which products are available for the client's own use at home?
   (d) What would be the effects on the hair shaft and skin of different products?
   (e) What after-care and guidance could you offer to the client?

3 How can you prevent cross-infection? Describe:
   (a) general hygienic measures to be taken;
   (b) action to take if disease is found *before* you have started hairdressing;
   (c) action to take if disease is found *after* you have started hairdressing;
   (d) advice you would give to a client found to have an infection;
   (e) action you would take after an infected client has left the salon.

Clynol

Conditioning and hair care

Hair care – principles

Caring for your client's hair and keeping it in good condition is the basis of good hairdressing. If the hair is torn and breaking, or the surface cuticle rough and splitting, the appearance will be dull and uninteresting. There may be loss of elasticity, and shape and curl will be difficult to hold. Control too becomes difficult. If you ignore poor condition and apply further harsh treatments, more serious damage may occur.

The client

☆ As a first step, consult the client. Ask what has been done and what has been used on the hair. If this is a regular client, check the record card for past history.

☆ Examine and analyse the hair and scalp closely. Assess the condition and extent of any damage to the hair.

☆ From what you can see, diagnose any problems – porous hair, loss of elasticity, cuticle peeling, split ends, dryness, etc. Try to find the reasons for these faults.

☆ Advise the client – what can be done, what treatments are available, which products to use, and the possible benefits.

☆ Agree with the client the course of action to be taken. Make sure that the cost of services you agree is acceptable.

☆ Make sure that the client is aware of the need for more than one treatment, application or process of conditioning.

☆ Emphasise the need for correct home care – offer advice and suggest ways the client can deal with the problem.

Possible problems

Hair condition is affected by many factors, including not just the external impact of chemicals, physical treatment and the weather, but also the internal effects of the client's health and lifestyle.

ACTIVITY

Visit your local chemist and list the different hair products that are available. You may be surprised at how many there are. Take note of the prices, the quantities, and the names of the manufacturers. Compare this range with your salon's own range of hair products.

ACTIVITY

Try drying several hair samples using a hand-held hairdryer, at 15 cm and 30 cm away from the hair. Compare the effects on the hair cuticle and appearance.

ACTIVITY

Using your hair samples, expose one to the sun, another to salty water, and another to chlorinated water collected from a local swimming pool. (First ask the attendant if you may take a sample.) Compare their effects. Then use the samples for conditioning, and again record your results.

External factors

These include all physical treatments, such as:

☆ combing, brushing, backdressing;
☆ shampooing;
☆ blow-drying/styling;
☆ hot rolling and brushing, crimping, or tonging;
☆ all hairdressing processes;
☆ wearing postiche, dreadlocks, etc.

Close examination of the hair and scalp is always necessary to check its state and condition. Look at the hair closely. Feel the hair's surface. Examine the skin of the scalp. Talk to the client, and listen to what is said. Ask what problems the client may have had.

Hair is subjected to many 'normal' treatments, such as shampooing. If badly carried out these can be the main cause of poor hair condition. If necessary, you should advise your clients on how to care for their hair at home.

Effects of the weather

These include:

☆ sun, wind, sand, sea and salt;
☆ extremes of climate – hot or cold, dry or humid;
☆ moisture effects on the hair's elasticity or flexibility.

If the effects of the weather are not guarded against, hair condition will inevitably become poor. In extreme weather it is best to keep the hair covered and protected.

Chemical effects

These result from:

☆ all hairdressing processes, including perming, tinting and bleaching, and **overprocessing** generally;
☆ swimming in the sea or in pools, if salt or chlorine is left on the hair and the hair is not rinsed thoroughly afterwards;
☆ the use of cosmetics, particularly where manufacturers' guidance is not followed.

If correct procedures are not followed, and the effects are not dealt with, further damage may result.

General health and lifestyle

The normal or abnormal working of the body has a direct effect on the hair and scalp.

☆ Good health is reflected in good hair and skin. A balanced diet with plenty of fresh foods contributes to good health.

☆ Disease, and drugs in medical treatment, take their toll on the hair and skin.
☆ Genetic factors affecting hair growth determine hair strength and texture.
☆ The hair of women in pregnancy is usually at its best. Deterioration of the hair and skin *after* giving birth is usually due to stress and tiredness.
☆ If hair becomes a focus of attention it may be pulled, twisted and in general handled too much.

Assessment

Close examination of the hair and skin may reveal the following states or conditions:

☆ dry/very dry, splitting hair, ends or shafts breaking, dull/very dull appearance;
☆ hair normal, smooth cuticle, shiny, easy to manage;
☆ greasy/very greasy, lank, difficult to control;
☆ dry, splitting ends with greasy roots;
☆ lack of elasticity, breaks easily (poor **tensile strength**);
☆ poor porosity (absorbs quickly but cannot retain);
☆ externally coated with chemical deposits from hairsprays, etc.

When you have assessed the hair condition, consider the treatments available to correct it. These are described in the rest of this unit.

ACTIVITY

Using some hair samples, apply different shampoos or conditioners and carefully note their effect on the cuticle, its elasticity and appearance.

Conditioners

The best **conditioners** protect hair so that it does not lose its natural condition, or help treated hair to return to a healthy condition. They have the following general effects:

☆ the hair cuticle is smoothed;
☆ hair tangling is reduced;
☆ broken areas of the cuticle or cortex may be repaired;
☆ the hair surface reflects more light, producing a gloss or sheen;
☆ surface acidity/alkalinity is balanced.

Conditioners may also be used to deal with particular problems:

☆ some allow the cortex to attract water – these are called **humectants** and **moisturisers**;
☆ others allow the cortex to retain moisture – these are called **emollients**;
☆ some counteract the effects of oxidation (chemical

ACTIVITY
Use some samples of hair in poor condition to try out various hair conditioners. Note the effectiveness of each.

reactions which take place during tinting, bleaching, etc.) – these are called **anti-oxidants**.

The following are some of the conditioners used:

☆ control creams, dressings, oils, hairsprays, gels;
☆ reconditioning rinses, emulsions, humectants;
☆ acid and alkaline rinses;
☆ restructurants and protein builders;
☆ anti-oxidants;
☆ pH balancers (after shampooing, tinting, etc.);
☆ gels, mousses (foams for setting, dressing, etc.);
☆ hair thickeners (for conditioning and building fine hair).

Kinds of conditioner

There are several different types of conditioner. Some remain on the surface of the hair, others penetrate the cortex. Some may be both surface *and* penetrating in their action.

Surface conditioners

Surface conditioners add gloss and help to make the hair manageable. They do not enter the hair but remain on the surface. They smooth the surface by coating it. Some also neutralise the effects of chemical processes such as tinting and bleaching.

Commonly used surface conditioners include:

☆ dressing creams and oils;
☆ reconditioning creams and lotions;
☆ acid or rehabilitating rinses.

These may be applied before, during or after treatments. They may contain some of the following ingredients:

☆ lanolin;
☆ cholesterol;
☆ vegetable and mineral oils;
☆ fats and waxes;
☆ lecithin;
☆ citric, acetic, and lactic acids.

Penetrating conditioners

Penetrating conditioners enter the hair shaft by capillary action – the passage of materials through the cellular spaces within the hair. Penetrating conditioners are designed to repair the chemical structure of fibres within the cortex which have been damaged or affected by previous hairdressing processes. These types of conditioner can also smooth the hair cuticle and make the whole hair structure much stronger. They may contain the following ingredients:

☆ quaternary ammonium compounds;
☆ sulphur compounds;
☆ protein hydrolysates (individual amino acids and very short lengths of polypeptide, prepared from animal proteins), which strengthen the hair;
☆ humectants, which hold water in the hair;
☆ emollients, which soften tissue and hair;
☆ moisturisers, which help to retain moisture.

Combined surface and penetrating conditioners

Both surface and penetrating conditioners may be combined with **bactericides** and **fungicides** to help stop the growth of bacteria and fungi on hair and skin.

How conditioners work

Modern conditioners achieve their effects by chemically balancing the hair structure. They also counteract the effects that chemical and physical processes have on the hair. This applies particularly to the alkalinity or acidity of the hair's surface.

The electrical and chemical properties of substances in conditioners help them to adhere to or combine with the hair.

Materials which are chemically attracted to the hair structure are called **substantive conditioners**. The newer **hair thickeners**, **hair builders**, **restructurants** and **protein hydrolysates** combine with the polypeptide chains within the hair, and create extra cross-links. This builds up the hair, and in some cases actually thickens it.

Protein hydrolysates are produced by a chemical reaction involving protein breakdown and the addition of water. They may be obtained from animal and other proteins. They are used in conditioners which strengthen and moisturise the hair.

ACTIVITY

With colleagues, examine and assess each other's hair condition before and after conditioning. Compare the effectiveness of different products and methods, and record your results.

Conditioning treatments

Conditioning treatments may be applied:

☆ to correct some hair states;
☆ to counteract the effect of hairdressing processes;
☆ as 'before' or 'after' treatments;
☆ to maintain healthy hair.

Dandruff

Dandruff, or **pityriasis capitis**, is caused by the overproduction of skin cells. It appears as small, very fine,

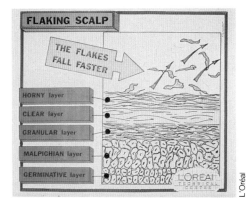

white, loose scales. These may irritate the scalp to varying degrees; they are also unsightly when they fall onto the shoulders, and may cause the sufferer anxiety. If the scales stick to the skin small patches of dry skin may result: these can cause inflammation.

Treatment

Dandruff is commonly treated at home. Treatment may include special shampoos, lotions or creams derived from tar, sulphur or zinc pyrithione. Recent reports suggest that fungicides may be helpful.

Special shampoos are usually sufficient, but particularly serious cases may require daily applications of anti-dandruff lotions or creams. If these are not effective, advise your client to see a doctor or trichologist.

It is important that you do not handle the hair roughly, and that you reduce scaling that might irritate your client's eyes. Although dandruff is not thought to be infectious, you should still take all the usual measures for hygiene to prevent any possible cross-infection.

Greasy hair

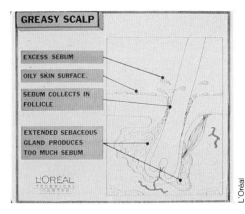

Greasy hair, or **seborrhoea**, is caused by grease from the sebaceous glands. These may be overstimulated by too much combing or brushing, or by too much hand or vibration massage. The use of greasy or oily products adds to the problem.

Treatment

Excessive grease must be removed by regular washing with balanced shampoos. Ammonium hydroxide, borax and astringent lotions may be used to correct excessively greasy conditions. **Astringent lotions** cause the skin to contract slightly, temporarily reducing the output of grease. If fungi or bacteria are irritating or stimulating the skin and causing the grease to be produced, fungicides and bactericides may be helpful, as may **alkaline rinses**.

These deal with the grease that is present: as with other problems, it is important also to identify the causes and deal with those too if possible.

Other hair conditions

☆ **Split ends (fragilitas crinium)** Treat with substantive conditioners or restructurants, and by cutting.
☆ **Damaged cuticle** Treat with restructurants, rehabilitating creams, etc.

Health and safety

When treating dandruff or greasy hair, try one product at a time. Give it time to work before trying something else.

- ☆ **Trichorrhexis nodosa** Treat with protein hydrolysates or substantive conditioners.
- ☆ **Dry, brittle, broken, overprocessed hair** Treat with rehabilitating creams, moisturisers, restructurants or protein hydrolysates.

These conditions may be caused by bad grooming, sleeping in rollers and curlers, wearing postiche too long, using poorly made combs and brushes, bad perm winding, chemical overprocessing, and overexposure to sun, wind and the like. Encourage your client to deal with the causes of the problem.

Where possible, cutting should be used to remove the worst areas of hair splitting.

Before and after processing

Where the cuticle has been damaged, the hair cortex becomes too porous, like a sponge, soaking up any chemicals applied to the hair. Older hair is more likely to be damaged than newer growth. The porosity must be reduced before hair will successfully take a perm or colouring.

Pre-perm treatments consist of lotions or creams that make porosity uniform throughout the hair, so that perm lotion will be taken up evenly. Pre-colouring treatments have a similar function, 'filling' or repairing areas of the cuticle. Use only conditioners that have been specially designed for use before chemical hairdressing processes, because these allow other materials to pass through to the hair – they are **permeable**. Conditioners that have not been designed to do this may form a barrier and make a process such as perming ineffective. Before using any conditioner, always check the manufacturer's instructions.

After processing, hair may need further treatment. For example, its normal state is slightly acid: many processes are alkaline, so an acid conditioner may be needed at the end to correct the pH. Acid balancers and anti-oxidants help to remove surplus chemicals such as hydrogen peroxide, and to smooth the hair and keep it manageable.

Maintaining a healthy condition

Keeping hair in good condition requires the regular use of conditioners to reduce the effects of harsh chemical and physical treatments.

Many poor hair states are caused by ignoring the basic principles of good hairdressing and grooming – cleaning and rinsing the hair correctly, carrying out processes as recommended, and handling the hair gently will all help to ensure good hair condition. Conditioners will keep healthy hair looking good and help in styling.

> **Tip**
> Before using any product, make sure you know what it does. Record the effects of each product on each client. Did it do any good? Did it cause any problems?

> **ACTIVITY**
> Compile a 'product knowledge' book: keep records of the different conditioners and treatments you use, and their effects on the different heads of hair. Don't forget those you use on your own hair!

Other treatments

The following treatments (with or without conditioners) may usefully be applied to the hair and scalp:

☆ massage;
☆ steamers;
☆ accelerators;
☆ rollerballs;
☆ radiant heat;
☆ oil treatments, shampoos and applications.

Massage

Massage is a method of manipulating the skin and muscles. It may be applied by hand or machine. In the salon you will apply massage to the scalp, neck and face only.

Effects of massage

☆ Improved blood flow to the skin – the redness this produces is called **hyperaemia**.
☆ Stimulation and soothing of nerve endings.
☆ Improved muscle tone, assisting normal contraction and relaxation.
☆ Removal of congestions or fatty lumps or adhesions in the skin.
☆ Improved removal of waste matter from the skin surface.
☆ Stimulation of the skin and of appendages such as hair follicles.
☆ Improved functioning of cells in the skin, including their nutrition, diffusion within them, and their ability to secrete substances.

There are several hand massage movements. The ones of special interest to hairdressers are effleurage, petrissage, tapotement, vibration, and friction.

☆ **Effleurage** A smoothing, soothing, stroking action, performed with firm but gentle movements of the hands and fingertips. You use it before and after most vigorous movements. It improves skin functions, soothes and stimulates nerves, and relaxes tensed muscles.

☆ **Petrissage** A deeper, kneading movement, used to break down adhesions or fatty congestions in the skin. It assists the elimination of waste products and the flow of nutrients to the tissues of skin and muscles. Gentle petrissage kneading movements are used on the scalp.

☆ **Tapotement** A stimulating tapping or patting movement –

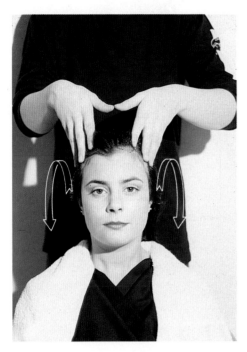

Effleurage

Petrissage

a rapid, gentle beating applied with the hands and fingertips. Tapotement is used to stimulate nerves, restore muscle tone, and free the skin of fatty deposits. It is *not* recommended for scalp massage – it is mainly used on the body, hands, and lightly on the face.

☆ **Friction** A rubbing movement applied with the fingertips in a light, flicking, gently plucking action. It is used on the scalp when applying lotions or during shampooing.

☆ **Vibration** A shaking movement, similar to friction but deeper. Light vibrations are soothing, heavier ones are more stimulating. These movements may be imitated by vibratory machines, commonly called 'vibros' and mainly used on the body. They *may* be used on the scalp, but only gently and carefully.

Friction

Points to remember

☆ Massage is only beneficial when applied in a quiet atmosphere. Keep noise and discussion to a minimum.

☆ Avoid hard, jerky, heavy movements to the scalp or head – this can only cause discomfort to your client.

☆ Complete massage should not take longer than 15 minutes. Overstimulation might cause a headache, muscle fatigue or other problems.

☆ Do *not* give massage if there are any **contra-indications** – inflammation, breaks in the skin, spots, rashes or signs of disease, or if the client is undergoing medical treatment.

Applying scalp massage

Scalp massage stimulates grease production and loosens skin, scale and dirt from the pores, so it is best given before shampooing. If the scalp or hair is very dirty, shampoo before *and* after massage. The duration of the massage depends on the client – some people can stand more stimulation than others. Older clients, for example, may be more sensitive.

A spirit-based massage lotion may help your hands and fingers to grip the skin surface. Remember that discussion between you and the client during massage will cause muscle tension to return, destroying the benefit of the massage.

1 Seat your client comfortably, with suitable protective garments.

2 Use effleurage first. Draw your fingertips firmly, but not too hard, over the head. Your hands should move from the front hairline down to the nape and shoulder tops.

Repeat this several times. Make sure that the whole scalp is covered in this way. This soothes the skin surface and the underlying structures, relaxing the client.

Tip

To prevent the kind of corrosion or scaling of the element and tubes that you find inside kettles and irons, use distilled water in steamers.

ACTIVITY

Place a dry hair practice block (or samples of very dry hair in poor condition) under a steamer, and steam for several minutes. Note how much more resilient, or elastic, the hair becomes.

A steamer

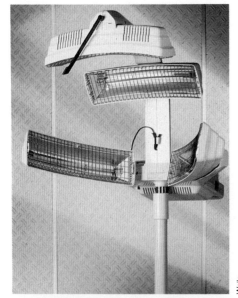

An accelerator

A rollerball

3 Next use petrissage. Apply this lightly but firmly: hard, fierce movements may rupture small blood vessels and cause discomfort.

With the fingertips, feel through the hair to the scalp, and gently rotate the scalp over the skull. To achieve and maintain the correct balance, pressure and movement, claw the fingers and move them towards the thumbs. Slowly and gently cover the whole scalp, without exerting too much pressure. Use the small fingers, particularly on the temples.

4 Finally, use effleurage again: this removes excess blood brought to the scalp.

5 Allow your client to sit quietly for a while, to enjoy the effects of the massage.

Steamers

Steamers are commonly used to apply moist heat to the skin and hair. They may be used before or during conditioning, and when tinting.

When you place the steamer over the client's head, steam is able to flow around the hair, which expands and softens. This helps conditioners to pass through the cuticle and enter the cortex of the hair. Conditioning products may be placed in the water reservoir and applied, with steam, to the hair. Steamers are beneficial when colouring and bleaching as they halve the normal processing time.

To achieve satisfactory results, always check the manufacturer's instructions before using the steamer.

Accelerators

Accelerators use radiated light and dry heat. They are useful for deep penetration of conditioning products. Like steamers, they help the hair to absorb conditioners and so reduce the processing time.

Rollerballs

The **rollerball** is a new kind of accelerator, using infra-red heat and also offering a fan. The source of the heat moves continually, preventing 'hotspots'. Hairdressing processes can be carried out while it is in use. The rollerball can be used while perming, colouring or treating the hair, or simply to dry it.

Radiant heat and infra-red lamps

Like accelerators, **radiant heat** and **infra-red** are used to irradiate the head and hair. The shorter rays of infra-red and radiant heat penetrate deep into the skin. Accelerators are used to activate certain chemical processes or to heat the hair before conditioning.

Oils

Oils are useful for conditioning very dry, overbleached or overprocessed hair.

Oil applications or treatments

These consist in the use of a vegetable oil (such as olive or almond) directly on the hair and scalp. Use a brush or cottonwool to apply the oil.

1 Pre-heat the oil to a comfortable temperature. Never use hot oil, as this is dangerous and could burn. Alternatively, apply heat to the hair using hot towels, heat lamps, a steamer or accelerator, before or after applying the oil.
2 Allow the oil to remain on the hair for 5–15 minutes. During this time you could apply a vibro massage.
3 Remove the oil from the head, first applying soapless shampoo: the shampoo combines (emulsifies) with the oil, and can then be rinsed off with water. Do not apply water first – it would prevent the shampoo from combining with the oil, so that after rinsing there would still be oil coating the hair and skin.

Oil shampoos

Oil shampoos are made from selected materials, with conditioning agents and emollients or tissue softeners. They are pH-adjusted; they regulate the acid balance of the hair (see Unit 4).

1 Use oil shampoos similarly to oil applications, heated as described above. You may apply hand or vibro massage while shampooing.
2 Remove the shampoo by rinsing with water, lathering, and finally rinsing the hair.

Paul Falltrick, for Clynol (photo: Ian Hooten)

Conditioning and hair care products

☆ After conditioning, the hair should be smooth, shiny, and with the cuticle repaired. It should look and feel better.
☆ The hair should be more pliable, more elastic and more resilient. Setting and styling should hold longer.
☆ There should be no tendency to tangle.
☆ Apply chemical processes only after careful testing – assess the condition thoroughly first.
☆ Read manufacturers' instructions carefully before applying conditioners or using equipment.
☆ Make sure the hair is towel-dry before applying

ACTIVITY

Look through the salon's client records. Note those of clients who have had illnesses. Have these clients experienced any ill effects after having hair processes such as perms and tints?

conditioners. Excess water could dilute them and reduce their effectiveness.

☆ Help your client to improve the home management of her hair – advise on home treatments that will help to maintain the improved condition, and when to return to the salon.

☆ For future reference, note on the client's record card details of conditioning treatments given.

☆ The client should be satisfied, and encouraged to return to the salon again.

Products

☆ **Shampoos** Many types are available – choose one to suit the hair's state.
Johoba For dry hair.
Soya For normal hair.
Orange For greasy hair.
Medicated For various hair types.

☆ **Setting and shaping agents**
Setting lotions, gels, mousses Used to hold or coat the hair when it is wet.
Plastics, PVP, other products Leave a film on hair; help to wet the hair thoroughly; resist the effects of moisture; reduce static electricity; help hair to hold its style longer.
Cationic detergents, cetrimide, and other products Keep hair pliable; repair damaged hair; reduce static; add shine.
Plasticisers, emollients, moisturisers Combine the features of other styling and shaping agents.

☆ **Hair thickeners and builders**
Cationic detergents Give 'body' to the hair.
Protein hydrolysates Attach to the hair and thicken it.

☆ **Conditioning rinses and agents**
Lemon juice (citric acid) Removes soap scum.
Humectants Ease combing; smooth the cuticle; counteract alkaline effects.
Vinegar (acetic acid) Removes soap scum; reduces alkaline effects; smooths the hair surface; eases combing.
Beer or champagne Add 'body'; smooth the cuticle; aid dressing.
Cream rinses or mousses Ease combing and brushing.
Cetrimide and other products Used after chemical processing – aid damaged cuticle; smooth the hair surface; act as anti-oxidants and pH balancers.

☆ **Restructurants**
Rinses, creams, gels or mousses, quaternary ammonium compounds, protein hydrolysates, proteins from soya and keratinous products Penetrate and aid damaged hair; soften hair; smooth the cuticle; add shine; make hair pliable and

able to hold shape; repair and fill hair structure; thicken
fine hair.

☆ **Anti-oxidants**
Rinses, lotions, creams Used after bleach and tints – stop
oxidation; neutralise alkalis.

☆ **pH balancers**
Rinses, lotions, creams Used after chemical processing –
counteract oxidation.

☆ **Dressings**
*Control creams, vegetable and mineral oils, gels and
gloss* Smooth the hair surface; soften the cuticle; retain
moisture; add shine; aid dressing.

☆ **Lacquers**
Shellac (hard coating), plastic (pliable coating) Resist
moisture, retain style/curl/shape, smooth the cuticle.

How to succeed

Checklist

In preparing for assessments on conditioning, the following list
may be useful. Check that you have covered and fully
understood these items:

☐ analysing different hair conditions;
☐ examining a range of conditioners and products, their
benefits and advantages;
☐ choosing and selecting suitable conditioners – for salon use
and for home use by the client;
☐ applying conditioners as recommended by suppliers –
before and after chemical processes;
☐ choosing and applying a variety of hair treatments;
☐ using massage (hand and mechanical), and knowing its
benefits and advantages, and any contra-indications;
☐ correctly applying suitable massage movements.

Self-check quiz

Oral and written questions are used to test your knowledge
and understanding. Try the following:

1 Which of the following helps to retain moisture?
(a) restructurant
(b) acid balancer
(c) lacquer
(d) humectant

2 Conditioners that are able to 'repair' hair are described as:
   (a) surface
   (b) temporary
   (c) substantive
   (d) emollient

3 The following neutralises bleaching effects:
   (a) a stabiliser
   (b) a moisturiser
   (c) an anti-oxidant
   (d) an emulsifier

Oral test

With the help of a friend, give spoken answers to the following:

1 Describe the causes of poor hair condition.
2 Name conditioning products for clients' use at home.
3 Give the meaning of each of the following terms:
   (a) humectant
   (b) contra-indication
   (c) restructurant
   (d) acid balancer
   (e) moisturiser

4 Describe reasons for combing and brushing hair correctly.
5 State the differences between hair conditioners.

Written test

Answer the following questions in writing:

1 With reference to hair condition, state:
   (a) the external factors involved;
   (b) the internal factors involved;
   (c) the various treatments of poor hair condition;
   (d) the difference between conditioners;
   (e) how hair can be maintained in good condition.

2 Describe scalp massage.
   (a) Name and describe scalp massage movements.
   (b) List the effects of massage.
   (c) Describe the sequence of massage movements for the scalp.
   (d) List the contra-indications.
   (e) List the precautions to be taken.

Shampooing

Shampooing – principles

Shampooing is an important procedure, which involves cleaning both the hair and the scalp. Shampooing removes dirt, grease and any other matter that coats the hair and scalp. This is essential in preparing the hair for other processes: if any deposits remain in the hair after shampooing, they may interfere with these processes – for example, they could block perm chemicals or leave the hair too greasy to blow-style.

The physical and psychological effects of good shampooing can be soothing, relaxing and enjoyable. Make sure your client is comfortable throughout. Poor shampooing may irritate your client, and lead to general dissatisfaction.

Before shampooing

☆ Discuss with the client what you are going to do.
☆ Select suitable protective clothing – gowns and towels.
☆ Analyse the state of hair and scalp, examining it carefully. Consider processes to follow. Ask questions, such as 'What products do you use at home?', 'How often do you shampoo your hair?', 'How do you style your hair?'
☆ Report immediately to a senior member of staff any signs of abnormality (disease or injury). Serious injury and some infectious diseases indicate that no hairdressing service should be carried out (see Unit 2).
☆ Consult with the client throughout. Make sure the client knows the price to be paid for any special treatments used, and agrees to your choice of shampoo.
☆ Indicate how long shampooing will take – about 5 minutes – and what is to follow.

Choosing a shampoo

Shampoos come in various forms, including creams, semi-liquids and gels. There are different shampoo bases (the

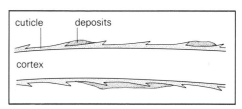

Dirt on the hair cuticle

Shampooing equipment

ACTIVITY

Try making your own conditioning rinses. Try a teaspoonful of lemon juice with 500 cl of water.

As a setting lotion, try 14 ml of beer. Use light beer for fine hair, dark beer for coarse hair. Note the absence of any smell when the hair has dried.

substances that form the bulk of the shampoo), some kinder and gentler on hair and skin than others. The detergent content in shampoos for greasy hair is higher than in those for normal or dry hair. The balance of the various shampoo ingredients, and their ability to deal with different hair types and conditions, is important.

Shampoos may be named after the ingredients contained in them, such as 'lemon shampoo' for its lemon essence or citric acid content. Herbal, vegetable and other natural products are popular.

Increasingly, hairdressers are using one basic, general-purpose shampoo for all types of hair. Such a shampoo does not contain special ingredients to deal with particular problems; instead these are treated afterwards with creams, lotions or other products. The method is thought to be more effective.

Popular shampoos

☆ **Johoba** For dry hair: contains a light non-greasy oil, which has good moisturising effects.

☆ **Coconut** For dry hair: contains an emollient, which helps to regain smooth and elastic hair.

☆ **Camomile** For greasy hair: brightens, shines, soothes; the dry powder is effective.

☆ **Rosemary** For normal hair: reduces scale, is antiseptic and stimulating.

☆ **Soya** For normal hair: contains a useful moisturiser.

☆ **Oil** For dry hair: contains pine, palm, almond and other oils; softens and conditions.

☆ **Egg** The egg white for greasy hair (it emulsifies grease and is easily rinsed), the egg yolk for dry hair.

☆ **Medicated** Helps to maintain the normal state of hair and skin; juniper is helpful if the scalp is scaly.

☆ **Treatment** Various shampoos, each designed to deal with a specific problem, such as dandruff or excessive greasiness: they usually contain cetrimide, selenium sulphide, or zinc pyrithione.

Making the right choice

The right choice of shampoo depends on several factors.

☆ *Type, texture and condition of hair* Fine hair requires a shampoo that will not degrease it or make it too fluffy. Choose a shampoo that will add body, or consider using a

ACTIVITY

When visiting a chemist or hairdressing wholesaler, note the shampoos that are recommended for frequent use (once or more daily).

Which types of shampoo does your salon use? Which does it sell for home use?

hair thickener. Coarse hair requires a shampoo that will tend to soften it and make it more pliable. Thick hair requires a shampoo that will penetrate and make good contact with all of the hair and the whole scalp. (Unit 3 discusses products designed to deal with hair in poor condition.)

☆ *Frequency of shampooing* If hair is washed once or more daily, choose a shampoo specially designed for frequent use.

☆ *Water quality* If the water used in the salon is hard, soap-based shampoos will tend to form scum. Use soap-free shampoos. In soft-water areas most types of shampoo can be used.

☆ *The function of the shampoo* Is it intended to colour, tone, condition or just cleanse the hair?

☆ *Hair treatments planned* What are you going to do with the hair later? Some shampoo ingredients (e.g. lanolin) coat the hair shaft. This would prevent cold perm lotions from working, for example. In this case you would need to use a pre-perm shampoo.

How shampoos work

The object of shampooing is to clean the hair by removing dirt, grease, skin scale, and sweat, plus any hairspray, gel, mousse, dressing cream, etc. Water alone cannot dissolve and rinse out all these substances to leave the hair in a suitable condition for processes such as blow-styling, setting, perming or bleaching.

Shampooing involves rubbing the head with shampoo and water to enable the cleaners to surround the hair and dirt particles. Using large amounts of shampoo is unnecessary and wasteful. A small amount, thoroughly spread and massaged into the scalp, is just as effective.

Types of shampoo

☆ **Soap shampoos** These are not generally used in salons nowadays. They cleaned the hair, but formed scum deposits on the hair and skin when used with hard water. These coated the hair and made it lank. Citric acid (from lemon juice) and acetic acid (from vinegar), made into rinses, were used to remove the scum.

☆ **Soapless shampoos** These are now popular in most salons. They are effective in hard and soft water, and do not leave scum deposits. The early soapless shampoos were very harsh and removed too much grease from the hair and skin. They also produced static electricity, which made the hair flyaway. These faults have now been largely overcome.

Tip
Regular brushing helps to remove dirt from hair.

ACTIVITY
Use a shampoo containing soap with hard water. Note the scum that forms.

Then use an acid rinse. Notice how the scum is cleared from the scalp and hair.

☆ **Synthetic detergents (surface active agents, surfactants)** The bases from which soapless shampoos are made. An example is **triethanolamine lauryl sulphate**, commonly known as **TLS**.

Detergents

By itself, water does not spread thoroughly over the hair and scalp. This is because water molecules are attracted together by weak electrical forces. These are particularly strong at the water surface, creating what is known as **surface tension**. On hair, water by itself tends to form droplets. The **detergent** in shampoo reduces surface tension, allowing the water to spread over the hair and scalp, wetting them. Detergents are described as **wetting agents**.

Each detergent molecule has two ends. One end (the *hydrophilic* one) attracts water molecules; the other (the *hydrophobic* one) repels them, and instead attracts grease. Detergent molecules lift the grease off the hair surface and suspend it in the water. The suspension is called an **emulsion**. The dirt is held by the grease, so as the grease is removed, the dirt loosens too. The emulsion and loose dirt can be rinsed away with water, leaving the hair clean.

A detergent molecule

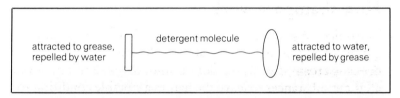

Detergent molecules surrounding grease

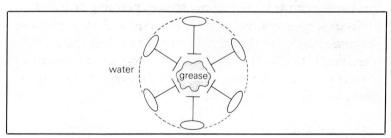

Shampooing technique

Apart from cleaning the hair, shampooing can affect the client's mood. Hands and fingers used too lightly or too harshly may irritate, as may missing out parts of the head. Be thorough in all your hand and finger movements.

Shampooing method

1 Protect and care for the client throughout the process.
2 First prepare the hair by combing and disentangling it.

Health and safety

Fingernails scratching or tearing the skin can cause discomfort and infection. Keep your nails smoothly filed.

Ensure that long hair is off the face and neck. Do not let it become tangled.

3 Check that the client is comfortable, especially the position of the head.

4 Run the cold water first, then mix hot water into the cold. Test the water mixture and temperature on the back of your hand. After lifting the spray, and before applying it to the client, test the water temperature again.

5 Check the water flow and pressure. Do not allow water to flow down the neck or onto the face.

6 Keep one hand between the head and the water spray – you will then be aware of any temperature changes.

7 Thoroughly wet the hair: avoid wetting the client.

8 Ensure that the hair, particularly if it is long, is controlled and directed into the water stream.

9 Apply shampoo, first into the palm of your hand. Distribute it evenly over the hair and scalp. Use as little shampoo as is necessary, or most of it will be wasted.

10 With clawed fingers, massage the scalp in a circular manner. Cover the whole scalp – be sure to avoid missing any part.

11 Rinse the hair thoroughly, again checking the water temperature and pressure.

12 If necessary, apply more shampoo and repeat the process.

13 Finally rinse all traces of lather from the skin and hair.

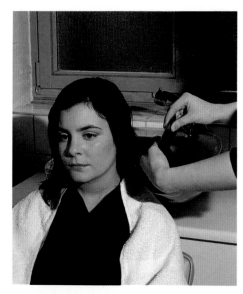

Disentangling the hair

Shampooing: water flow (*above*)
Shampooing: finger positions (*left*)

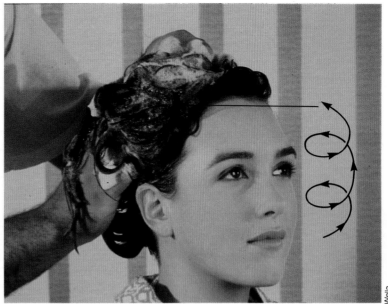

Wella

Massage

There are three types of massage movements you can use when shampooing: effleurage (stroking), petrissage (kneading), and friction (rubbing).

1 Begin shampooing with smooth effleurage movements.
2 Continue with firm but gentle petrissage movement:
   □ Let your fingertips glide over the scalp. Lift your hands periodically to avoid tangling the hair.
   □ Move your hands towards each other – up from the sides to the top and down across the nape area.
   □ Move your hands in decreasing circles around the head to make sure you cover the scalp fully.
3 Use lighter, plucking, friction movements to stimulate the scalp gently.
4 Finally, use soothing effleurage movements to complete the shampooing process.

While shampooing

☆ Make sure the client is comfortable at all times.
☆ Check massage movements, water temperatures, water flow and pressure, and the client's position.
☆ Work hygienically. This is good practice at all times; it also reassures your client who can then relax and enjoy the hairdressing processes.

After shampooing

1 Turn off the water flow. Return the spray head to its place.
2 Lift the hair from the face. Wrap it with a towel, and gently

---

ACTIVITY

With colleagues, shampoo each other's hair. Compare the shampoo action with long and short hair.

Massage the scalp. When the hair is long, notice the position of your hands. How often do you lift the hands from the head to avoid tangling the hair?

remove any surplus water remaining in the hair.

3 Reposition the client comfortably.

4 Check that all shampoo, dirt and grease has been removed and that the skin and hair are clean. (Your assessor or trainer will be specially looking to see whether the hair and skin *are* clean after shampooing.)

5 At this stage you may apply conditioner if this is required.

The hair should now be ready for combing and the processes to follow.

Health and safety

Raising a client from a forward washing position too quickly can result in dizziness. Allow a little time before moving a client to another position.

Do not let the hair fall over the client's eyes when moving.

Remember that, apart from chilling or scalding your client, water that is too hot or too cold can cause shock. Always check the water temperature before applying the water.

After shampooing

Do's and don'ts

☆ Give complete attention to the client.

☆ Never use unwashed linen on another client.

☆ Ensure that towels and gowns are clean, in place, and not too tightly secured.

☆ Use sensible hygiene to prevent cross-infection and to safeguard health generally.

☆ Do not allow shampoo to come into contact with the client's eyes.

☆ Direct the water flow away from the client to avoid wetting the clothes and face.

☆ Comb the hair after shampooing, without tugging or pulling it.

☆ Immediately after use, clean the part of the salon where the shampooing was done. Remove dirty, used towels. Replace shampoo containers. Make sure the chair is left clean.

☆ Always turn off the water – do not allow water to run continuously between washes. This soon empties the hot water tank. By turning water off when it is not in use you avoid delay, waste, and higher costs.

☆ Always rinse your hands after shampooing. Do not allow shampoo to remain: it might cause dryness and soreness. Gently pat your hands dry – never 'scrub' them with a towel.

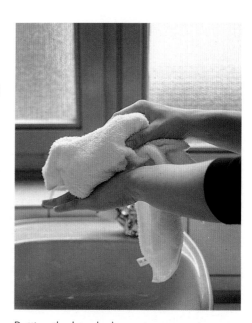

Patting the hands dry

Water for shampooing

Salons use a lot of water – about 10–20 litres for each wash. It is therefore important that there is a constant supply of both hot and cold water. Anything that interferes with the salon's plumbing and drainage systems may cause delay and financial loss. Don't leave hot taps running longer than necessary, or you will soon empty the hot water tank.

Cold water reaches the salon via a main supply pipe from the road: if necessary this can be disconnected using a **stopcock**. Cold water is stored in a tank. Some is heated (using gas, electricity or oil) and stored in a second, hot water tank.

Waste water leaves the salon via outlet pipes to the drains. Beneath each basin is a **waste trap**. This has two functions. First, it holds water and stops gases and smells from the drains reaching the salon. Second, it collects hair and debris, making the pipes less likely to block. If an earring, for example, falls through the plughole, you can retrieve it by undoing the trap.

Hot water storage and supply (*right*); plumbing and drainage (*far right*)

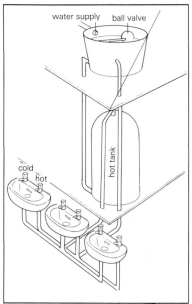
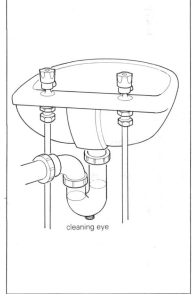

Retrieving an earring from a bottle trap

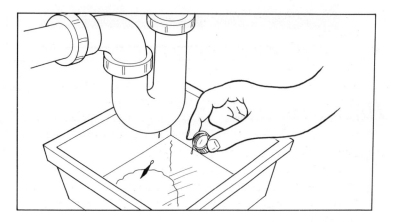

The pH scale

Shampooing, like other chemical actions, can affect the surface of the skin. You should consider how acid or alkaline the skin surface will be left after shampooing.

The **pH scale** measures acidity or alkalinity. It ranges from pH 1 to pH 14. **Acids** have pH numbers below 7. **Alkalis** have pH numbers above 7. **Neutral** substances have a pH of 7. The *higher* the pH number, the more *alkaline* the substance; the *lower* the pH number, the more *acid* the substance.

The normal pH of the skin's surface is pH 5–6. This is referred to as the skin's **acid mantle**. The acidity is due in part to the sebum, the natural oil produced by the skin.

An important skin function is the protection of the underlying tissue (Unit 2). The skin does this by acting as a barrier, preventing liquid loss from inside, and keeping excess liquid outside the body.

It also protects the body from infection. An acid skin surface inhibits (slows down) the growth of bacteria, and makes them less likely to enter the skin. If the acidity of the skin is reduced – if the pH rises above 5–6 – infections are more likely. This may happen if the pH is not adjusted after chemical hairdressing processes such as perming.

The pH can be tested using pH papers. **Litmus papers** will tell you whether something is acid, alkaline or neutral.

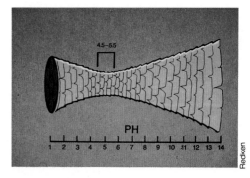

The pH scale

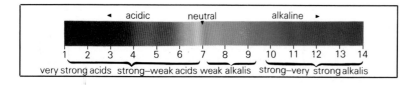

How to succeed

Checklist

In preparing for assessments on shampooing, the following checklist may be useful. Check that you have covered and fully understood these items:

- ☐ considering and determining the client's requirements;
- ☐ examining and noting the present hair state;
- ☐ considering chemical processes to follow;
- ☐ selecting and choosing suitable shampoos;
- ☐ discussing and advising on products for the client's home use;
- ☐ applying shampoo;
- ☐ applying massage;
- ☐ achieving effective shampooing.

Self-check quiz

Oral and written questions are used to test your knowledge and understanding. Try the following:

1 'Scum' is a product of hard water and:
   (a) a detergent
   (b) a soap
   (c) a surfactant
   (d) a shampoo

2 Shampooing water temperatures should be tested:
   (a) before washing
   (b) throughout shampooing
   (c) after washing
   (d) after shampooing

3 The following is a suitable shampoo ingredient for dry hair:
   (a) johoba
   (b) egg white
   (c) camomile
   (d) rose water

Oral test

With the help of a friend, give spoken answers to the following:

1 What guidance can you offer clients on the use of shampooing and conditioning products?
2 Describe the correct position of fingers and hands when shampooing.
3 How often should hair be shampooed?
4 What types of shampoo are available?
5 Which shampoos should not be used before chemical processes?

Written test

Answer the following questions in writing:

1 With regard to shampooing, describe:

(a) the position of the client;
(b) what shampooing does;
(c) the correct shampooing movements;
(d) how the hair should be rinsed;
(e) how to look after the client afterwards.

2 With reference to soapless shampoos, describe:
   (a) the alternatives;
   (b) the advantages of each;
   (c) the main differences between shampoos;
   (d) what is meant by wetting action and surface tension;
   (e) what is meant by detergency.

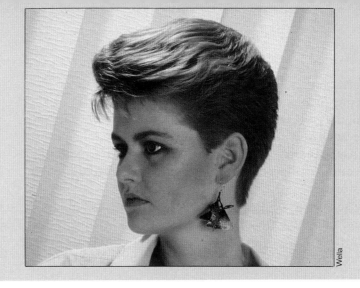

UNIT 5

Hair styling and cutting

Hair styling – principles

Hair styling is the creating or designing of attractive hair shapes or arrangements. It involves competent cutting, setting, blow-drying and dressing.

A **hairstyle** is an expression of form and shape. It is achieved by arranging the hair into suitable, balanced lines, which complement the shape of the head and the facial features.

The aim of the style is to enhance your client's appearance. This helps to boost her confidence and make her feel good. There are styles for work, play, special occasions, business meetings, parties and so on. The hairstyle should be considered a part of the complete **ensemble**, including the clothes, make-up, and accessories.

The client

☆ Make sure you have protected your client's clothes adequately.

☆ Before attempting a new style, communicate with your client to be sure that you are in agreement.

☆ Discuss what is required and make sure that you consider all your client's needs, including her general lifestyle.

☆ Examine the hair type, length, colour, quality and quantity – all can influence the hairstyle. Look at how the hair has been cut previously, and decide whether there is enough hair for a change of style.

☆ Analyse the client's requirements and requests. Beware of requests for named styles: what is called one thing by the client may mean something completely different to you! Make sure you interpret your client's wishes correctly.

☆ Assess the limitations. Do not make the mistake of being persuaded to cut hair into a style you are sure would not suit your client.

☆ With your client, select the style. Many clients are swayed in their choice of style by the attractive, youthful and pleasing pictures of young models in magazines. If you think the style favoured by the client is unsuitable, tactfully suggest an alternative. Not giving the client exactly what she has requested should not be the result of your whim, bias or incompetence, nor a wish on your part to dominate the situation.

☆ Advise the client how long cutting will take – anything from 15 minutes for a trim to one hour for a complete restyle.

☆ Agree with the client how much hair should be taken off.

☆ Help your client by advising how to manage the hairstyle at home successfully.

☆ Reassure the client afterwards – the resulting style, if new, may need getting used to. If your client is not immediately pleased with the result, don't be disappointed but keep your comments positive. Others will soon compliment the client on the hairstyle, and boost her confidence.

Andrew Collinge, for TRESemmé

Choosing a hairstyle

The hairstyle you choose with your client must be designed to suit the following:

☆ the shape of the face and head;
☆ the features of the face, head, and body;
☆ the dress and occasion for the style;
☆ the quality and quantity of the hair;
☆ the age of the client;
☆ the way the hair grows, its position, proportion and form in relation to other styling requirements.

The shape of the face and head

This is the base on which the hairstyle will rest. The proportions, balance and distribution of hair should relate to the underlying structure and **features**. Use features such as the eyes, nose and chin as a guide to the finished style.

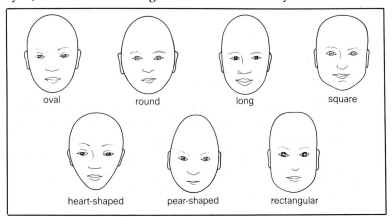

oval   round   long   square

heart-shaped   pear-shaped   rectangular

Faces and head shapes

If you look at the outline of your client's face, you will see that its outline is quite individual – round, oval, oblong, heart-shaped, square, etc. An oval shape is considered ideal as most hairstyles fit it.

☆ The *apparent* length of square and oblong faces may be accentuated by sleek, flat styles, or diminished by full sides.

☆ A large, round face looks even rounder when the hair is full and foaming around it; it looks longer when dressed high at the front and less full at the sides.

☆ Hard-looking shapes, resulting for example from prominent jaw bones, appear harder when hair is dressed back, but softer with forward hair movements.

☆ The roundness or flatness of the head shape and the profile – the side view of the chin, mouth, nose and forehead – affect the look of the style.

☆ The neck – its length, fullness and width – directly affects the fall of the back and nape hair.

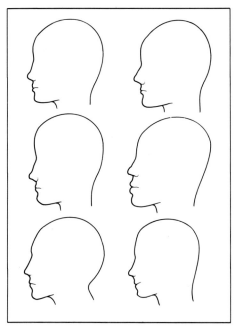

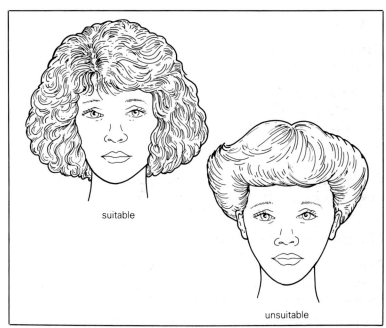

suitable

unsuitable

Profiles (*above*)
A correct and an incorrect style for a
heart-shaped face (*above right*)

Features of the face, head and body

☆ Note the size, shape and characteristics of your client. The way the head and body are held is important – you can see this best when you first receive the client.

☆ A prominent or large nose may be 'diminished' by dressing the front hair at an angle, or avoiding a central parting.

☆ Square jawlines may be softened by fuller side dressings; protruding ears are best covered.

☆ Double chins are exposed if hair is taken away. A longer, fuller dressing may be helpful.
☆ Wrinkled eyes are made more obvious by straight, hard-line dressings. They may be diminished by softly angling the hair away from the eyes.
☆ Low, high, wide or narrow foreheads may be disguised by angling the hair and varying fringe positions.
☆ A large, fussy style on a big person can look unsightly. Yet a small, head-hugging style may be completely out of proportion.
☆ High-dressed styles accentuate height. Flat styles make short people look shorter.
☆ The shape of facial features – the line and shadows cast by them – should be used to counterbalance the hair bulk, and enhance or soften overall features.
☆ Spectacles and hearing aids will influence your choice of style. Keep hair off the face and away from spectacle frames. Bring hair over the ears to disguise hearing aids.

Dress and occasion

The dress and occasion for which the style is to be worn will help you decide on a suitable hairstyle.

☆ A style suitable for a special occasion may differ from one worn at work: a beautiful evening gown requires an elegant hairstyle, normal working clothes may require a smart and unexaggerated hairstyle.
☆ Many clients require styles that are practical and easy to manage. Practicality is less essential for special events, but remember that the hair has to be returned to normal after the event.
☆ Particular jobs require particular hairstyles – nurses and canteen workers need to wear their hair off the face and shoulders, and many people wear hats as part of their uniform. Do not choose a hairstyle that makes this difficult.
☆ Usually, lower necklines require longer hairstyles. Higher necklines allow higher dressings. There are exceptions – dancers and ice skaters will not want loose, flowing styles that will impede movement or vision.
☆ Models require specific and often elaborate hairstyles for demonstrations or photography.

The quality and quantity of hair

☆ Poor condition and texture never look attractive and will not style well. Shining, healthy hair is essential for good styling.
☆ Thin, scanty hair is difficult to manage and requires

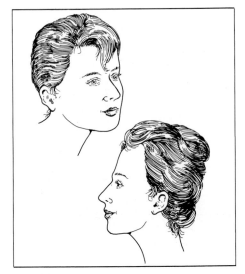

Facial features

Hairstyles complementing dress

attention. Styles which make it appear thicker and fuller are usually successful.

☆ Very fine, thin hair is soon affected by damp hair and loses its shape. Use setting aids, hair thickeners and practical styles.

☆ Dry, thick hair requires sleek, smooth, styles to contain it. This hair type soon fluffs and loses its shape. A control dressing (a cream, gel or spray) may help.

The age of the client

Men and women of different ages require different styles.

☆ Children require simple hairstyles that don't require much dressing at home. Shorter styles often suit younger children best.

☆ Young men and women can take most styles. Good, often odd, effects are used by this group. Straight or curled, long or short, hard or soft effects may be used to advantage. A younger client may want a style that is unique and individual, or something 'trendy'. Teenage fashion tends to exclude styles worn by older men and women. The more extreme glamorous styles are generally requested by young women.

☆ Young career women generally go for fashionable styles which they wear as part of their everyday dress. Such hairstyles need to be practical and easy to manage as well as fashionable.

☆ Older women require greater consideration for suitable styling. Facial features – lines, wrinkles and double chins – need to be 'styled out' (made less obvious).

☆ Young businessmen may require the smart, well shaped, perhaps less extreme styles favoured by teenage boys.

☆ More mature men require usually flattering or classic, practical shapes, generally less 'fussy' and easier to manage than women's hairstyles.

☆ The use of colour in men's styles – apart from the more fashion-conscious – is generally more reserved. Subtle shading or toning is more applicable.

Hair position, proportion and form

☆ The outline formed by hair in relation to the shape of the face contributes to the overall effect.

☆ Dressing of the hair varies this outline. It is important that you maintain balance between hair and face.

☆ Consider hair growth directions or distributions – strong movements and natural partings, hair streams, hair whorls, cowlicks, widows' peaks, and double crowns. Make allowances for these when cutting and dressing, and particularly when designing the style.

Tip

The more the unwanted features are highlighted, the less suitable the style will be. The most suitable style is one that is individually designed.

☆ Hair growth patterns and the way the hair falls or moves is best seen when the hair is wet. Hair styling can disguise the natural position and form of the hair.

☆ A good hairstyle follows the natural fall and growth of the hair, and will not lose its shape easily between visits to the salon.

☆ Cutting a nape whorl too short produces difficulties – the hair may stick out in all directions.

Styling requirements

You will often come across the terms *suitability*, *balance*, *line*, *movement*, *soft and hard effects*, and *originality*. You should understand what these terms mean, so that you can choose different hairstyles with confidence.

Suitability

Suitability is the effect of the hair shape on the face, and on the features of the head and body. A hairstyle is usually suitable when it 'looks right'. This is achieved when the moulded hair shape fits the other shapes of the head. A line of the face may be accentuated when the hair lines are continuous with it. It may be softened when they are angled away.

A young, fashionable style dressed on an older woman may be unattractive. This is because the lines of the face, eyes and forehead are accentuated by the harder lines of 'younger' styles. Most fashion styles are designed for younger women and must be adapted if they are to meet the needs of older women.

Balance

Balance is the effect produced by the amount, fullness and distribution of hair throughout the style. **Symmetrical**, 'even' balance is achieved when the hair is similarly placed on both sides of the head. **Asymmetrical**, 'uneven' balance is achieved by, for example, dressing long hair on one side of the head and countering the weight with one earring on the other. Here the lines and proportions created by the dressing produce the 'balanced look'. A good hairstyle should be balanced from all angles of view.

Hairstyle with balance

The line of the style

Style **line** is the direction, or directions, in which the hair is positioned. It should 'flow' throughout the shape. If the line suddenly ends, the style becomes unbalanced and the wrong effect is produced.

The line of the style is affected by the way it fits in – or fails

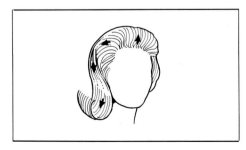

Hair direction and flow of hair

to fit in – with the features and contours of the face. It should carry the eye of the viewer along the directions in which the hair is placed. Many style lines produce **illusionary effects** by accentuating or diminishing different facial features.

Partings have a strong effect – a long, straight, central parting appears to make the nose more prominent. A short, angled parting 'diminishes' a prominent nose. Round, fat faces appear larger with central partings and smaller with side partings.

Movement

Movement is the name given to varying directions of style line. The more varied the line, the more movement there will be. Curly or wavy hair displays movement. Style line should move from one point of the head to another in a fluid fashion reaching to the ends of the hair. Styles with movement are usually complimentary to older women.

hard line
(Egyptian)

soft line
(classical Greek)

Hard and soft effects

Soft and hard effects

Soft and hard effects depend on balanced lines and movements. Hair dressed without divisions, without sudden line variation and without any abrupt finish to the movement looks natural and soft. Careful colouring enhances soft effects – careless colouring produces hard, unwanted effects. Lack of movement and irregular, unbalanced shapes together produce hardness. Rhythmical movement and balancing are softening.

Originality

Creating completely new style lines requires a great deal of thought and work. You can adapt styles and fashions to create interesting and sometimes original variations. Displays, demonstrations and competitions offer more opportunities for original hair styling. Whatever hairstyle you choose, it should be designed for the individual client.

Types of hairstyle

You need to be able to cut and dress hair in a range of styles to meet the requirements of different clients. The following are some in general use:

☆ **Day styles** should be attractive, uncluttered and easy to manage, without extreme ornamentation, colour or elaboration.

☆ **Evening styles** are generally more elaborate, not necessarily practical, and suitable for special occasions. They are usually augmented with colour or ornament.

☆ **High fashion (haute coiffure)** refers to the latest style trends. At first they may appear to be extreme; they became more acceptable when better understood. This type of styling requires originality, good techniques, and experience.

☆ **Fashion styling** (usually adapted from high fashion) is favoured by the smart and trendy. There seems to be an endless round or range of fashions stimulated by events, advertising, dress designs, etc.

☆ **Children's styles** should be natural and suitable, never artificial – in general, the simpler the better.

☆ **Men's styles** are based on principles similar to those that apply to women. They should be natural, balanced and suited to the client's face and features.

Equipment and safety

You have considered the 'artistic' part of hairstyling – choosing a style to suit your individual client. Now you need to consider the practical part – the tools used for cutting, how to use them, some points on safety, and the terms and techniques used in cutting into style.

Cutting tools

Tools should always be clean, sharp, and well balanced. They should fit the hand and feel comfortable in use.

☆ **Scissors** with straight or curved, and long or short blades may be used. They should never be too heavy, nor too

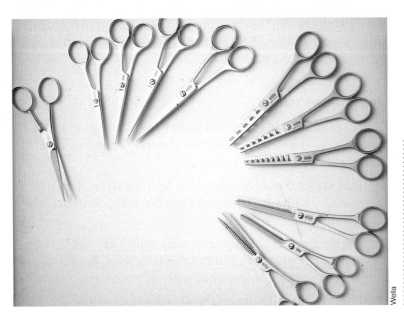

Wella

ACTIVITY

Visit a hairdressing wholesaler. Note the different types of cutting tools and their prices. You will see that there is a great variety of scissor lengths and weights. It is important that scissors and other tools are comfortable to use. Ask a senior or your tutor to advise you on the best tools to purchase.

Scissors: their parts, and how to hold them

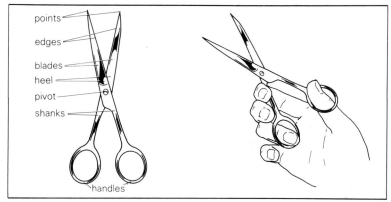

long, to control. Since scissors need regular resharpening, you will need at least two pairs, preferably of the same type.

The best way to hold a pair of scissors is with the thumb through one handle and the third finger through the other. This ensures ease of use, good control, and little effort. It also minimises stress on your hands, arms, back and body.

☆ **A razor** – the open, 'cut-throat' type – consists of an edged steel blade protected by the handle. A solid or hollow ground blade may be used for cutting hair or shaving. Modern counterparts are called **hair shapers**. The modern razor-like hair shaper has a replaceable blade and a protecting handle. There are other types and shapes.

With the handle open, the thumb and index finger hold

A razor, and how to hold it

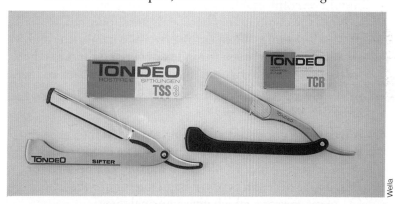

A hair shaper, and how to hold it

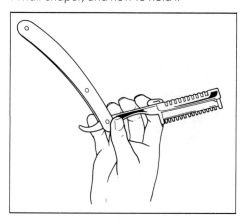

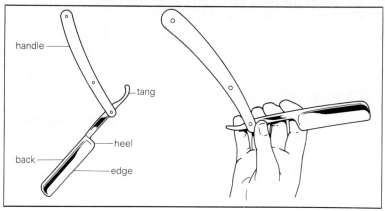

the back of the guarded blade, between the pivot and the tang. The two middle fingers rest on the tang, on either side of the handle. The guard restricts some razoring movements; this may be overcome by using shorter strokes.

☆ **Thinning scissors** have one or both blades serrated. The size of the serrations determines the quantity of hair that is removed at each cut: the more often they are closed on the hair section, the more hair is removed. They may be held in the same way as cutting scissors, but are used in an opening and closing fashion. They cannot be used in a slithering action.

☆ **Clippers** – both hand and electric (the latter are becoming more popular) – consist of two blades, with sharp-edged teeth. The blades are positioned such that one blade remains static and the other moves across it. Hand clippers are operated by pushing the handles together; electric clippers are operated by a motor. The distance between the blade points and the spacing of the teeth determine how closely the hair can be cut.

☆ **Combs** suitable for use while cutting are thin and pliable, with both fine and coarse teeth. Fine teeth allow the hair to be controlled and closely cut. Coarse teeth allow for repeated combing and positioning of the hair. The comb should be comfortable in use and easily positioned.

Hold the comb so that both ends are supported, to prevent breaking. When cutting over the comb, one end should be held between the index finger and thumb – the finger on the teeth edge and the thumb on the back of the comb. As the comb is turned, so the finger and thumb grasp the back of the comb.

☆ **Mirrors** are important while cutting so that the shape can be seen clearly from different angles. The client, too, will want to see the final result: hand mirrors can be used for this. Three different types of hand mirror are available:
  ☐ *plane* mirrors, which give a normal view;
  ☐ *concave* mirrors, which magnify;
  ☐ *convex* mirrors, which give a smaller, distant image.
The plane mirrors are commonly used in the salon.

Cleaning cutting tools

☆ Never use dirty or broken tools. Germs breed in the many corners and may be transferred between clients.
☆ Clean all tools before disinfecting or sterilising. Remove all loose hairs. Use spirit or alcohol to remove any grease.
☆ Special disinfectant oils may be used to lubricate moving parts.

Health and safety

The disposable blade or razor is now recommended for general use.

Health and safety

Do not use clippers if the top, movable blade protrudes beyond the bottom, static blade – you might cut or damage the skin.

plane mirror – reflection appears the same size

concave mirror – reflection appears larger

convex mirror – reflection appears smaller

☆ Some disinfectants corrode metal and blunt edges – check the manufacturers' advice before using them.

☆ If corrosion or rusting occurs, light rubbing with emery paper helps to restore the metal surface. Badly marked tools may be corrected by professional servicing.

☆ Scissors and razors are easier to clean than clippers. Hand clippers can be dismantled. It is not advisable to take electric clippers apart, though some clipper heads are removable for cleaning.

☆ All repairs should be carried out by the manufacturers, or by qualified electricians.

☆ All clean and sterile tools should be stored in a dry disinfectant cabinet, or at least covered.

Dangers and precautions

☆ Examine the hair and scalp thoroughly – signs of disease indicate that you should not proceed with cutting.

☆ Do not place sharp tools in overall pockets – this is unhygienic and dangerous. You might cut your hands, or stab yourself when bending.

☆ Allowing loose, cut hair to gather on the floor is unsightly, dangerous and unhygienic. It is easy to slip on loose hair.

☆ Take care not to cut yourself when replacing shaper blades or using razors.

☆ Do not use clippers with broken teeth – they can pull, drag or tear the scalp.

☆ Use only tools that are sharp, to prevent splitting or breaking hair.

☆ Beware of clients moving suddenly, particularly children. Watch out for a sneeze – you might stab your client!

☆ Clean tools after use and store them in a safe place.

ACTIVITY

In case of accidents at work, or someone being taken ill, it is important to know what to do. Try to take a first-aid course so that you are prepared for any emergency.

First aid

If skin is cut, take the following action:

1 Bathe the area with cool water.
2 If it is a minor cut, apply antiseptic and cover with plaster.
3 If it is severe, apply pressure to stem the blood flow. If bleeding does not stop, seek medical help as soon as possible. If necessary, treat your client for shock.
4 Avoid contact with blood, to prevent cross-infection.
5 Wash and disinfect any bloodstained surfaces.

Cutting and styling technique

Cutting hair to fit the shape of the head is one of the most important hairdressing processes. It forms the basis of all hair shapes and styles. When a client washes her own hair, the cut shape is what remains. The cut affects the way that the hair lies on the head and influences all other hairdressing processes. A well-shaped head of hair should be pleasing to look at and easy to manage.

Terms and techniques

When different people use particular terms they don't always mean the same thing. Below is a list of useful terms, with explanations of what they mean in this book.

Tapering

Tapering or **taper cutting** means reducing hair so that it tapers easily to a point. It may at the same time be used to shorten the hair.

☆ **Scissor tapering** – used on dry hair – is a slithering, backwards-and-forwards movement along the hair section. The hair is cut in the heel of the blades from the third of the section that includes the points.

☆ **Razor tapering** – used on wet hair – achieves a taper effect. The razor is placed, at a slight angle, on or under the hair section. The hair is cut in a series of slicing actions. The length may be reduced at the same time. Cutting should be restricted to the third of the section that includes the points.

☆ **Point tapering** achieves a taper effect by using the scissors points to remove hair from the point ends of the hair section.

☆ **Feathering** is another name given to tapering. It also describes the overall effect of dressed, tapered hair.

☆ **Backcombing taper** achieves its effect by first backcombing a section of hair. The points ends remaining in the hand are then tapered with a sliding, slithering action of the scissors or razor. The amount of backcombing determines the degree of taper.

Clubbing

Club cutting or **clubbing** is a method of cutting hair sections bluntly, straight across. It reduces all the cut hairs to the same length. It may be used on wet or dry hair. If too large a section is clubbed the resulting line of the hair ends will be irregular. You need to cut small sections of hair at a time.

☆ **Scissor clubbing** – of wet or dry hair – is the most common. Small slicing actions ensure a clean cut.

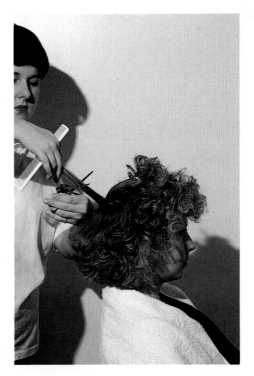

Cutting: tapering

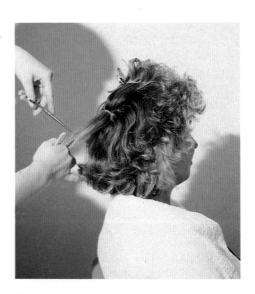

Cutting: point tapering

Cutting: clubbing

ACTIVITY

Using hair samples that are naturally curly, note the effects of clubbing, tapering and thinning on the curl strength.

Cutting: texturising

Thinning

Thinning reduces the length of some of the hairs in a section without shortening the hair overall. The hair's bulk is reduced. Hair is cut at the middle third of the section – if cuts are made too close to the scalp, thinning will cause short stubble to stick out.

☆ **Scissor thinning** is achieved with scissors used in a long tapering action. It can also be achieved by deep backcombing and tapering, or by point cutting at the middle third of the section.

☆ **Thinning scissors** have serrated blades. When closed onto a section they thin it automatically. Cuts should be made at the middle third of the section and towards the points.

☆ **Razor thinning** reduces thick bulky hair. Make long slicing cuts from mid-lengths to the hair points. Use little pressure or you will cut through the section.

☆ **Modern hair shapers** with removable blades are used in short, sharp movements to thin hair. The blade is angled slightly and cut from mid-section to points.

☆ **Root thinning,** with scissors or a razor, is achieved by cutting small hair sections level with the scalp. It is a drastic method, rarely used on the average head: it is used in some fashion and competition styles.

Producing varied lengths

Texturising, castle serrations, slicing, chipping and **chopping** are terms used to describe methods of varying lengths of hair within a section. They also describe the look of the cut hair, which gives the effects of some hairs being lifted and supported by others.

☆ **Castle serrations** are produced with special serrated scissors which drastically reduce parts of the hair section. The amount of hair to be removed is determined by the style effects required.

Wet and dry cutting

Wet and dry cutting refers to methods of scissor or razor cutting. *Scissors* may be used on wet or dry hair. Scissor tapering should not be used on wet hair as the action of the blades is restricted. *Razors* and *modern shapers* are commonly used to taper or thin wet hair; they are never used on dry hair as they drag and tear it, cause pain to the client, and blunt the cutting edges. *Clippers* and *thinning scissors* are best used on dry hair.

Graduation

Graduation is the difference in length between the upper and lower layers of a section of hair. It is the slope produced, from longer to shorter hair, by the ends of the hair.

If a section of hair is held out at right angles to the head, and cut at right angles to the section, the hair will lie evenly on the head. The angle of the cut and the contours of the head together make the ends lie neatly over each other, producing a graduated curve (**uniform layering**). This may best be achieved by clubbing.

☆ **A graduated cut** can be produced by clubbing the hair, to make it short in the neck graduating to long at the crown, or longer at the nape and shorter at the crown.

☆ **Reverse graduation** refers to a graduated line being shortest at the lowest layers and longest at the higher layers. This is used where the hair is required to 'turn under', as in some long or short 'bob' styles.

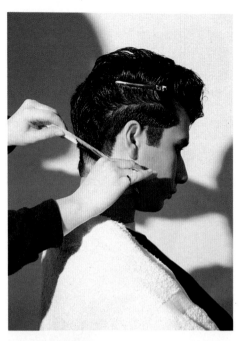

Cutting: graduation

Layering

Layering is the term given to the process of cutting sections of hair to similar lengths. It produces a uniform, unbroken shape. A uniform layer can be produced by holding hair sections out at right angles to the head and cutting across them at right angles.

'Layering' is also used to describe thicker and more distinct layers, cut directly into the hair shape. These layers are *not* uniform: there is a sharp difference in section length.

Controlling the shape

☆ **Angles** must be considered when you are applying any method of cutting. Two in particular are important:
  □ the angle at which the hair section is held out from the head;
  □ the angle at which the cut is made across the hair section.
  By varying these two angles you can produce a wide variety of effects.

☆ **Cutting lines** are the lines formed by the hair *ends* when combed out from the head. The two main cutting lines to consider are:
  □ the contour of the head from side to side, often called the **outer perimeter line**;
  □ the contour of the head from front to nape, often called the **inner perimeter line**.
  Both these contour lines must be followed during any cutting.

Cutting: reverse graduation

Tip
When cutting, always use part of the previously cut hair as a guide to cutting and shaping the next part.

Cutting: layering

Cutting: angles

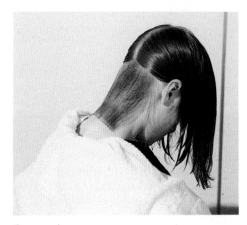

Cutting: lines

☆ **Guides** for cutting are specially prepared sections of hair. These are cut so that both the length and the cutting line are fixed and visible. The guide can be followed throughout the cutting process to produce even and precise results. Cutting haphazardly, without guides, produces peculiar and unwanted effects.

To prepare guide sections you should carefully note the features of the head – the position of the eyes, ears, nose, hairline points, etc. Further guides may be prepared in the neck, at the sides, and at the front, to be followed throughout the cutting process.

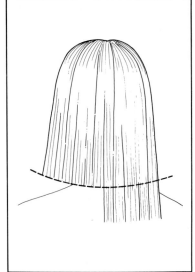

Cutting: guides

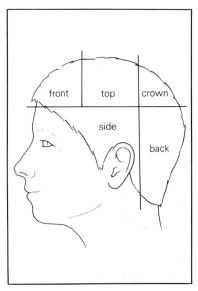

Cutting: guide sections

> **Tip**
>
> It is important to consider the amount of hair that will be left on the head after cutting. The closer the cut is made to the head, the more hair is removed.

Cutting practice

To a certain extent, you can learn and practise tool movements and positions, combing hair at different angles, control of hands, hair and so on before you start cutting. Use practice hairpieces (**slip-ons**) which slip over a block. These allow your first cutting attempts to be monitored by your supervisor. You will soon be able to practise on live heads.

Cutting for the first time can be successful if you use a simple pattern and take a slow, methodical approach. You will only achieve speed in cutting after lots of practice. Never cut fast at the expense of a good hairstyle.

Fashion style cutting

This involves cutting hair to a particular shape, and requires a variety of techniques and methods. To create pleasing and unique effects, you should follow a carefully prepared pattern of cutting. This must be based on the elements of styling.

Cutting the lines and angles

Comb the hair and hold neat sections of it away from the head. The position in which you hold and cut the hair determines the positions the cut sections take when combed back onto the head.

ACTIVITY

Using hair samples, practise the various haircutting techniques. Sketch the effects or shapes produced with each of the hair samples. Note the effect on the samples when trying to curl or wind them.

Tips

A section of hair held out at right angles (90°) to the back of the head, and cut at right angles (90°) to the section, produces a 45° angle of graduation. This describes the gradient between the top and bottom of the hair section when positioned back on the head.

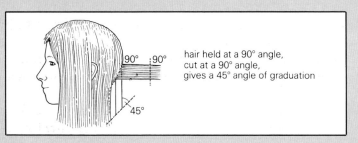

hair held at a 90° angle,
cut at a 90° angle,
gives a 45° angle of graduation

A section of hair held at 90° and cut at a 45° angle produces a steeper graduation.

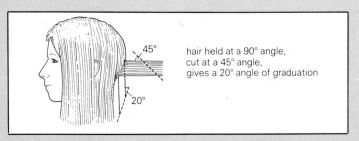

hair held at a 90° angle,
cut at a 45° angle,
gives a 20° angle of graduation

A section of hair held at 90° and cut at a 145° angle produces a 'level length', in which all the ends of the hair fall level, without graduation.

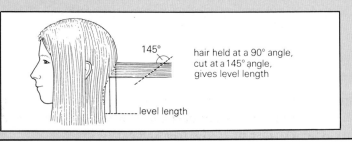

hair held at a 90° angle,
cut at a 145° angle,
gives level length

level length

Tip

It is important to follow the contours of the head, and the cutting lines must match the outline, the shape and the lengths required.

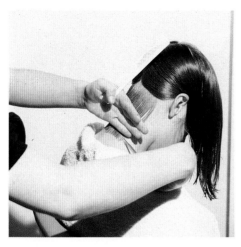

Cutting: perimeter lines

The angles and lines of cutting vary with the different lengths required by the style. The first cutting line – the *outer perimeter line* – may be determined in the nape, as well as determining length. The second cutting line – the *inner perimeter line* – varies with the different lengths required throughout the style.

General style cutting

Although the methods of cutting you use may vary, the end results should not. Whether cutting horizontally, vertically or diagonally, or any combination of these, the hair should fit the head. There should be no visible steps, broken curves or lines, unless these effects are actually required. The finished cut should not need to rely on blow-drying, setting, or dressing for its shape – you should use these techniques only to enhance and position the cut hair.

☆ A good approach to cutting is to choose a suitable starting point, providing yourself with a clear, visible guide for continuous cutting lines. This will help you to cut the hair easily. Be sure that all guide sections – particularly the first – are accurate so that following sections fit correctly. Consider carefully which techniques to use – tapering, clubbing, cutting the hair wet or dry, using scissors or a razor, etc.

☆ Make sure throughout that you hold the client's head in suitable positions, so that you achieve the required shape.

☆ When sectioning hair, take sections that are small enough to hold comfortably. If the sections are too big, you will not be able to control your cutting and the result will be inaccurate.

☆ At the end, show the hairstyle to your client. Hold the hand mirror behind her at an angle, so that she can see the back and sides of her head reflected in the large mirror in front of her.

One-length shapes

The one-length shape, or **bob cut**, involves the top layers of the hair falling into a line level with the underlying layers. With the weight of the hair on the outside, the ends can be made to turn under. The term **level length** is commonly used.

A bob can be produced as follows.

The nape

1 Section the hair and make sure that the lengths and weight are clipped away from the nape. Sub-section into a position in which the hair can be seen and cut easily.

2 The first cut determines both the outer perimeter line and the length. First comb and hold the centre nape hair, then cut it.

3 Successive cuts should follow a line passing from one side of the nape to the other. (Use the ears as a guide – 12 mm below each ear may be suitable for shorter lengths.)

4 Take a section (12–18 mm) of the nape hair. Hold this horizontally between two fingers, the fingers resting on the neck. Using scissors, club this section in a smooth, slicing action, making several cuts.

5 Working on either side of this first cut, make a series of further cuts. The cutting line should follow an unbroken curve from ear to ear. Each new section taken along this line should overlap a previous one, so that a part of the previously cut hair can be clearly seen.

6 When complete, the cut nape hair serves as a guide to the cutting of the other sections and layers of the back hair.

The back

7 The next section, above the nape, should be about 12 mm deep, depending on the thickness of the hair. Comb it down, sub-divide it, and then cut it as you did the underlying nape hair. Remember not to stretch the hair or pull it too tightly; if you do, the hair will retract above the nape line and will be uneven. It is better to cut the second section of hair slightly below the first cut nape sections.

8 Allow the cut hair to remain in its natural position so that following sections can be cut in line with it. If you cut the hair out of its natural fall or position, the shape may be distorted when the hair has dried.

The sides

9 Comb the first section at the base of the side, and hold it horizontally between the fingers. Line it up with the cut nape hair, then cut it to continue the curve round to the side. Do not hold the hair too far away from the head or you will produce graduation. Do not pull the hair tight, either, or make it flatten the ear. Make allowance for the hair to lie over the ears without 'shrinking' when dry.

10 The higher layers of the sides may now be sectioned and cut using the previously cut hair as a guide.

The fringe

11 The process of cutting the fringe depends on the type and shape required. The fringe area covers the top front of the head.

Cutting: stages in a bob cut

Completed bob cut

Fringe cutting

12 Section and comb the hair forward onto the forehead. The perimeter line can be cut to a variety of shapes. Then cut the upper sections, placing them onto the lower, previously cut, sections. It is important to determine the type and texture of shape so that the correct techniques – such as feathering, chipping or clubbing – can be used.

In a successful bob cut the ends of the hair fall evenly. The client's position throughout the cut must be maintained to avoid distorting the level and shape.

Reverse graduation, in which the top layers are longer than the underlying ones, is a commonly used technique. It encourages the hair to turn under. It produces full, swinging hair, which should return naturally to its position.

Uniform layers: inner lengths same as outer lengths

This cut ensures that all sections of hair are cut to the same length throughout. It is known as a **short, layered cut**. It can be long or short, but is more commonly used for short styles. If you use this cut on longer hair, the top layers will fall over the lower ones, producing a degree of graduation.

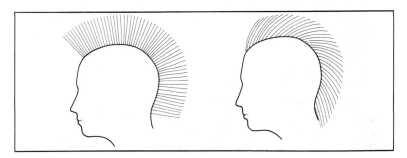

Cutting: same lengths

The nape

1 Section the nape hair and cut the length, and the first part of the perimeter line, horizontally.
2 Cut the inner line by sub-dividing the nape hair and taking the sections vertically.
3 Hold the hair directly out from the head at 90°, and cut it at 90° to the section. This gives uniform lengths.

Cutting: inner line

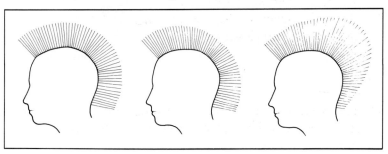

The back

4 Each of the higher sections is then sub-divided and cut vertically only. The lower, previously cut sections are used as a guide.

The sides

5 Treat the sides similarly. Cut the perimeter section horizontally and then vertically – this ensures that both the outer and the inner perimeters are shaped.
6 Are the sides to be dressed back or forwards? Angle and cut them accordingly.

The fringe

7 Fringes may be cut by combing the hair forward. Determine the length and shape by reference to the nose, eyes, eyebrows, and other features of the face.

Uniform layers: inner lengths longer than outer lengths

This cut can be used to produce a shorter shape in the nape sections and longer layers at the crown. The nape can be cut very short, the length graduating to the longer lengths of the upper layers. The terms **shingling**, **semi-shingling** and **Eton crops** have been used for this style of cut; now it is known as a **graduated-wedge cut**. The cut can be varied, depending on the hair lengths required in the nape and crown.

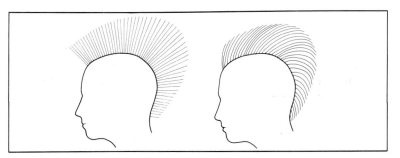

Cutting: inner layers longer

The cutting method

1 The method follows that for the short, layered cut, except that as the sections are sub-divided and cut vertically the angle of cut is changed. Hold the hair section out at 90°, and cut the hair across at 45° to the section. This gives longer lengths in the layers.
2 Use the same angle of cut throughout, so that as the layers are allowed to fall back onto the curve of the head, a soft, unbroken line of graduation is achieved. Harsh lines and

divisions may be produced if this is not carried out correctly.

Uniform layers: inner lengths shorter than outer lengths

This cut, the **long, layered cut**, may be used to produce shapes with longer nape hair (a longer outer perimeter) and shorter layers on the higher and inner perimeter. You can use this cut for a variety of shapes, depending on the lengths produced. Softness may be suggested by the longer lower lengths and by the fullness around the lower ears and jawlines.

Cutting: inner layers shorter

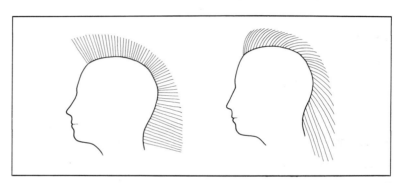

The cutting method

1 Section and sub-section the lower nape hair. Taking a small section, usually mid-nape, cut the first part of the outer perimeter line horizontally.
2 Re-comb the section and hold it out from the head at 90°. Cut the hair at 145° to the section. Then use this as a guide while cutting the hair above.
3 Take down this upper hair in approximately 12 mm sections. Carefully cut it on the previously cut sections of hair, leaving longer nape hair with the upper hair getting gradually shorter.

Necklines

These may be shaped in various ways. They may be cut curved, straight or pointed, or graduated high or low. Low graduation produces soft effects. When cutting above the natural hairline, be careful to avoid harsh effects. Where hair is cut shortest, particularly at the nape, make sure that hair growth patterns do not distort the effects required.

Trimming

This is a term used for the removal of small amounts of hair. It is usually done to retain the original cut style. To reproduce the

Cutting: neckline shape

original shape, use similar techniques, cutting lines and angles to those used for the original cut.

Restyling

To **restyle** is to design a completely new hair shape. You need to check that the hair is long enough for the style requested. Some styles require certain lengths, and it may take time for the hair to grow before these can be achieved. If your client is particularly keen to have a certain style, you may need to work on it gradually over several months, for instance to allow earlier layering to grow out.

How to succeed

Checklist

In preparing for assessments on cutting and styling, the following list may be useful. Check that you have covered and fully understood these items:

- [ ] determining clients' needs and requirements;
- [ ] advising on suitable, and possible, styles;
- [ ] deciding and agreeing on the final cut, shape and style;
- [ ] applying techniques – clubbing, tapering, thinning, etc.;
- [ ] taking care and considering the client throughout cutting;
- [ ] completing one-length bobs, layering cuts, graduations, etc.;
- [ ] achieving client satisfaction with the cut and style produced.

Self-help quiz

Oral and written questions are used to test your knowledge and understanding. Try the following:

1 Which of the following techniques reduces length only?
   (a) tapering
   (b) thinning
   (c) clubbing
   (d) slithering

2 Well-designed hairstyles are:
   (a) expensive
   (b) suitable
   (c) impractical
   (d) unsuitable

3 Hair-length difference between upper and lower layers is described as:

(a) texturising
(b) graduation
(c) chipping
(d) shortening

Oral test

With the help of a friend, give spoken answers to the following:

1 Name some haircutting guides.
2 Define each of the following terms:
   (a) balance
   (b) suitability
   (c) hard and soft effects
   (d) face shapes
3 What hairstyles would suit round and square faces?
4 Describe clubbing and tapering techniques.
5 Why should you hold cutting tools correctly?
6 Describe the considerations that affect cutting and styling.

Written test

Answer the following questions in writing:

1 Consider cutting and styling. State:
   (a) what must be discussed with the client, and the examination required;
   (b) what must be considered before cutting;
   (c) the sectioning methods used;
   (d) the cutting guides and angles used;
   (e) the dangers, and precautions to be taken.

2 With regard to hair styling, state:
   (a) what must be taken into account;
   (b) what is meant by line, movement and suitability;
   (c) the different types of hairstyles;
   (d) a definition of *haute coiffure* and fashion style;
   (e) advice and after-care to be given.

Goldwell

Blow-styling

Blow-styling – principles

Blow-styling is the process of styling wet hair while blow-drying it. Using a hand-held dryer, you use a variety of techniques to create different effects. While directing heated air onto the wet hair, you mould the hair with brushes, combs, or your fingers, positioning the hair to fit the style for which you have cut it.

Like other methods of setting wet hair (see Unit 7), blow-styling works by changing the hair's structure. When wet, hair can stretch up to 50 per cent of its length. Heat softens it. The weaker links between the polypeptide chains (the hydrogen and salt bridges) are broken, allowing the keratin to stretch from its alpha to its beta form. While wet, and by applying heat, hair can be moulded into a chosen shape.

The styled shape is only temporary, though – as the hair gradually absorbs moisture from the atmosphere, it returns to its original state. Combing styled hair with hot water returns the hair to its natural form straight away.

Heat moulding techniques

Heat can be applied to hair in other ways: to wave it, using irons; to curl it, using tongs; to crimp it, using heated crimpers; or to straighten it, using hot combs or hot brushes.

Like other methods, these techniques depend on the softening effect of heat. The moulded hair must be allowed to cool before it will hold its shape – if you comb through it while it is still warm you will lose or distort the shape. Hair moulded in this way returns to its natural state if combed with hot water.

The client

☆ Prepare the client by removing wet towels and making sure that she is comfortable.

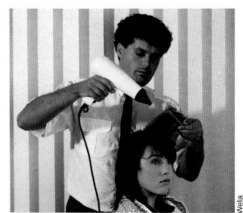
Wella

Blow-drying

☆ Before you begin work, communicate with your client about her requirements.

☆ Diagnose what can and should be done.

☆ With the client, discuss what should be done and why. The client, especially if new, will find this reassuring.

☆ Make sure the client understands and agrees with the final effect you are trying to achieve.

☆ Analyse the technical requirements at this stage, in the light of your overall plan.

☆ Indicate how long the process will take – generally about 20–30 minutes for blow-styling.

☆ Monitor and evaluate your work as it progresses. Make sure your client is satisfied and reassured throughout.

☆ Explain to your client how to achieve a similar style at home.

Blow-styling technique

The technique you choose will be determined by the hair texture, the quality and quantity of hair, the style to be produced, and the cut. The most suitable hair for blow-styling is firm, thick, coarse hair. There are now a number of styling aids – thickeners, setting mousses and gels – which are designed to give direction to the hair. Fine, fluffy hair requires the help of one of these if you are to obtain successful results.

The following techniques are commonly used in blow-styling:

☆ **Blow-waving** Shaping the hair into waves, using directed heated air from a dryer, and combs, brushes or your hands. It achieves natural, soft fullness.

☆ **Blow-drying** Simply drying the hair with the hand-held dryer. It is usual to blow-dry hair into a chosen shape, or in a required direction.

☆ **Scrunch drying** Gripping and squeezing clumps of hair, while directing heated air into the hand. The process yields a casual, ruffled, moulded shape.

☆ **Finger or hand drying** Lifting, teasing, pulling and directing hair with the fingers or hands. Casual, soft and full shapes can be achieved. Bellowing fullness is perhaps the chief effect.

☆ **Blow-combing** Drying and shaping using a comb, or a comb attachment fixed to the hairdryer. It is a kind of blow-drying, and achieves shape and direction.

☆ **Blow-stretching or straightening** A means of smoothing, unkinking or straightening the hair. A variety of brush shapes and sizes may be used.

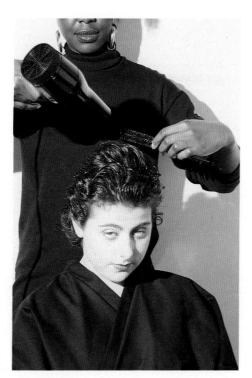
Blow-styling

A **blow-style** consists of first shampooing the hair, then softening it with a dryer or heated lamp, and finally moulding it into shape using a blow-dryer. It may be dressed, if required, when the hair has cooled.

Equipment

☆ The **hand-held dryer** is the most important piece of equipment you need. There is a wide range of models to choose from. The dryer should have adjustable speeds and temperatures, and be designed for long periods of use. It needs to be light and easy to hold, and to have controls positioned where they are easy to reach when in use. There should be a means of attaching it safely to the bench when not in use.

Blow-stretching

Goldwell

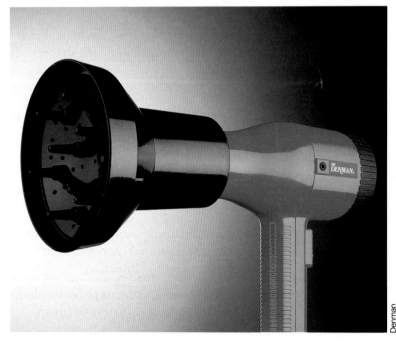

Denman

Hand-held dryer with diffuser

ACTIVITY

At your wholesaler's, look at the different types of hand-held hairdryers. Professional models are designed for continual use in the salon. Compare these with the hairdryers available in the shops, which are designed for home use. Clients often ask which is the best dryer for home use: what would *you* answer?

☆ **Hand dryer attachments** – such as nozzles and diffusers –
are available. The nozzle helps to direct the heated air with
greater force. The diffuser lessens the direct force and flow,
and is used for finishing styles. (Using the dryer without a
nozzle or diffuser allows for a wider directed air flow.)

☆ **Brushes** are probably the most important items after
blow-dryers. A firm, stiff, bristle or plastic brush is
required. This will help you to grip, direct and control the
hair. (Soft brushes are suitable only for finishing.) Half-
round plastic brushes are used for general shaping. Larger
types are best used on long hair, smaller for short-to-
medium hair. A range of smaller roller brushes on which to
form shapes is also required. Different brushes are
necessary for particular shapes.

☆ **Combs** should be professional and heat-resistant. The
comb you will use most will have both widely-spaced and
narrowly-spaced teeth.

> ### Health and safety
> Metal combs retain heat and can burn the skin.

Preparing hair for blow-styling

1 Shampoo and towel the hair dry, then comb out any
tangles.
2 Cut the hair into style.
3 Apply a suitable blow-styling aid, such as mousse, gel or
lotion, if required.
4 Section the hair – the longer the hair, the more sections you
will need.
5 Clip long hair out of the way and re-section it as required.
6 Position and grip the hair with a brush, a comb or your
fingers to control it.

Blow-drying

You can start blow-drying at any part of the head. On long
hair it is best to dry the lower, underneath sections first. With
practice you will achieve a continually moving brush
technique, with the lift and control required. Do not allow the
top sections, which are still wet, to fall onto the lower,
previously dried ones: this spoils work done and wastes time.
Clip wet hair well out of the way.

Blow-styling is best on coarse hair. Fine hair may quickly
become overheated and overdried. When dealing with short
hair, take care not to blow it out of line. The air stream should
be directed the way the hair is intended to lie. Short hair may
be best rolled onto a circular brush, allowed to cool, and
combed or dressed into position.

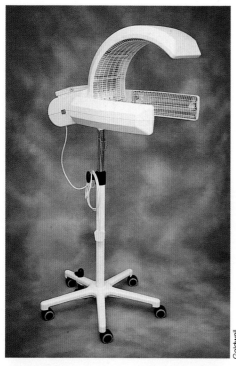

A heat lamp

Brushes

> ### Tip
> Always dry the roots first, before
> the middle and end lengths of the
> hair. If you don't do this, the hair
> won't lie in the direction of the style
> you intend.

Which tool or technique you use depends on the style effects required. For full, soft effects use large, round brushes. For more bounce and curl, use smaller brushes. Fluffy effects may be achieved with open bristle brushes. A general method is as follows:

1 Towel-dry the hair. With hands and fingers loosely stroking and lifting the hair, remove any excess moisture. Apply mousse or blow-drying agents, if required.

2 Cleanly divide small sections of hair. The angle to lift the hair is determined by the fullness required. Lift the hair to allow the heated air to penetrate the section. For one-length, bobbed shapes, take sections horizontally or diagonally. For swept-back shapes, use vertical sections.

3 It is important to work methodically and cleanly. Make sure that the hair *not* being dried is clipped up, so that it doesn't get in the way.

4 Place the sectioned hair onto the brush with the thumb or fingers. When the hair is firmly in position on the brush, begin directing heated air onto it – first on one side of the section, then on the other. With the brush, direct the hair section away from the head so that the root ends are thoroughly dried. Do not wind the brush right down – allow space for the hair to be dried. Keep the brush moving as the heated air is passed repeatedly over the section, winding the hair up and down to allow the warm air to penetrate the hair fully. Make sure each section is fully dry before passing on to the next.

5 Allow the hair to cool before removing the brush – when warm, it is still soft.

6 For maximum lift hold the hair section well up from the scalp. Keep the dryer close to the hair but moving, and directed away from the scalp. This action should be for short periods of time. Generally, hold the dryer about 300 mm from the hair. For wedge shapes, blow air through the hair section as the hair is allowed to flick from the brush in a combing, lifting action.

Scrunch drying

1 Prepare the hair for blow-drying, by removing excess moisture with a towel, or hood drying the loose hair.

2 Run the fingers through the hair and lift it from the scalp.

Scrunch drying

ACTIVITY

Select three textured practice blocks of different hair and blow-style each in a very full style. Leave them in the salon where they can absorb atmospheric moisture. Note how long the different textures of hair hold their shape and position.

As you lift it, grip it firmly. Direct the heated air into your hand just before closing your grip. Hold the hair firmly and continue drying.

3 To see the effect produced, tousle the hair by shaking it. It is important to follow the shaping process in the mirror.

4 Continue to direct the hot air into the palm of the hand, to prevent discomfort. Repeat the process of blow-drying, gripping the hair, and lifting hair sections, to increase volume and shape.

5 Work from side to side. Make sure each section is dry before proceeding to the next.

Providing the shape is carefully studied, a full, lightly tousled effect can be produced by this method.

Hand or finger drying

This is similar to scrunch drying, but uses hands and fingers to lift, mould and shape the hair. It gives a wider, looser, billowing fullness.

Blow-waving

A method of waving using a comb or brush, carefully directed heated air, and a series of shaping movements. Position the hair into a crest formation and direct heated air through a nozzle attachment. Control the waves by comb or brush movements in relation to the hair position. Repeated combing or brushing is required to shape the hair.

Finger drying

1 Begin at the front hairline and follow the hair's natural movements.

2 With the wide-toothed end of comb, make a backward, slightly turning movement, gripping the hair and holding it in a wave-crest shape.

3 Direct warm air onto the trough below the crest. The airstream should be opposite to the direction of the comb holding the hair. The airstream should be at half strength, or the hair will be blown away from the comb.

4 Movements of both hands must be co-ordinated and repeated. Continually move the dryer along the hair. This directs the heat evenly and avoids burning the scalp.

5 The second crest is formed similarly to the first. Direct the airflow along the line the hair is intended to lie. This produces the required line and shape. When you reach the hair ends, position them in line with the waves formed.

6 Use of the coarse end of the comb allows air penetration and speeds the process. For finishing, use the fine end. A smooth finish can be obtained by lightly blowing through a net stretched over a frame.

Health and safety

Do not try to blow-wave when the hair is too dry or wet. Keep the airstream moving, to prevent discomfort.

Blow-combing

This is a drying method using a **blow comb** – an electric comb with heated jets of air flowing over, or between, spaced teeth. You can use it to dry hair loosely or to produce wave shapes in long hair. Either pass the comb repeatedly through the hair, or hold the hair in position to form wave shapes.

Blow-stretching or straightening

This involves the technique of stretching the hair rather than waving it. The aim is to straighten and smooth the hair lengths. Use larger, round brushes under or on sections of hair, and turn them to grip and slightly stretch the hair. This technique produces soft, slightly lifted shapes on very short hair, and sleek straightness on long hair. The brush size must be varied to suit different lengths of hair. Use a hand-held dryer, as in blow-drying, and direct the heated air onto the stretched hair. This technique is equally suitable for both women's and men's hairstyles. You may also use heated combs for straightening hair.

Precautions when blow-styling

- ☆ Use only professional tools.
- ☆ Ensure that all electrical equipment is in good order.
- ☆ Never use electrical equipment with wet hands – you might be electrocuted.
- ☆ Never use faulty equipment.
- ☆ Work comfortably – avoid continually twisting or stretching the body.
- ☆ Maintain high standards of hygiene.
- ☆ Test the heat of the dryer before applying it to the hair – you may cause discomfort to your client or damage to the hair. If the air is too hot for the skin, it is too hot for the hair.
- ☆ Direct hot air away from the scalp.
- ☆ Do not keep the dryer in one place too long.
- ☆ When straightening, never overstretch the hair.
- ☆ Do not attempt to shape hair when it is too wet.
- ☆ Tugging and pulling the hair may cause breakage.
- ☆ Use suitable blow-styling aids, such as lotions and creams, to protect the hair from overheating.
- ☆ Do not blow-style hair that is in poor condition.

Dealing with complaints

If your client does not like the style you have produced, the following may help:

Styling products

Tips

Make sure the filter on the hairdryer is cleaned regularly – if blocked it could damage the dryer.

Don't hold the dryer too close to your body. If you do it will pick up fluff from your clothes, which may block the filter.

Don't rev the dryer motor – this eventually causes it to overheat and fuse.

☆ Take steps to rectify the complaint as soon as possible.
☆ Try to see the client's point of view and be sympathetic in your response.
☆ Explain that the new style requires time to adapt to.
☆ Honestly justify what you believe is correct and suitable.
☆ Do not talk the client into something that you do *not* believe is suitable.
☆ Do not allow the client to leave with a poor shape or style.
☆ It is relatively simple to rectify a blow-style by re-dressing, re-setting, wetting the hair and blow-drying it again, etc.
☆ Exercise tact, understanding and courtesy throughout.
☆ Most clients do not like to express displeasure and may become distressed. Be aware of this, and make sure your client really is satisfied.

How to succeed

Checklist

In preparing for assessments on blow-drying and blow-styling, the following list may be helpful. Check that you have covered and fully understood these items:

☐ determining a suitable blow-style for your client;
☐ discussing the possible limitations of hair type, condition, etc.;
☐ explaining the techniques, sequence of movements, etc.;
☐ applying the different techniques for styling;
☐ checking the safety of all the tools you use;
☐ ensuring that tools are kept clean;
☐ using disinfectants safely;
☐ completing long hairstyles in about 45 minutes;
☐ completing short hairstyles in about 30 minutes.

Self-help quiz

Oral and written questions are used to test your knowledge and understanding. Try the following:

1 Blow-styling effects are:
   (a) permanent
   (b) temporary
   (c) semi-permanent
   (d) long-lasting

2 Lifting, gripping and squeezing hair when blow-styling is called:
   (a) blow-drying
   (b) finger drying

(c) scrunch drying
(d) straightening

3 Blow-styling mainly affects the following hair content:
(a) cortex
(b) disulphide links
(c) keratin
(d) melanin

Oral test

With the help of a friend, give spoken answers to the following:

1 How does blow-styling affect hair structure?
2 What are the precautions to be taken when blow-styling?
3 Name some blow-styling techniques.
4 Name some blow-styling aids.
5 Which hair texture is best for blow-styling?

Written test

Answer the following questions in writing:

1 Consider the process of blow-styling. Describe:
(a) the methods and techniques;
(b) a blow-drying procedure;
(c) a blow-combing procedure;
(d) techniques of hair straightening;
(e) precautions to be taken when blow-drying.

2 Consider the effects of blow-styling on hair structure. Describe:
(a) the texture and condition of hair that is unsuitable for blow-styling;
(b) the changes in the hair structure;
(c) the difference between scrunch and finger drying;
(d) the difference between blow-styling and setting;
(e) the safety factors to consider when blow-drying.

UNIT 7

Setting

ACTIVITY

Using sketches or photographs, compile a style book. Collect those styles that appear to you to be suitable and complimentary to the wearer. Also collect hairstyles that are totally *unsuitable*, and note why you think this is. Discuss these styles with your colleagues and tutors.

Setting – principles

Like blow-styling, **setting** is a method of drying wet hair into shape. It can be used to produce a range of effects – you can make hair straighter, curlier, fuller, flatter or more wavy.

Setting involves placing wet hair in chosen positions, and holding it there while it dries into shape. You may roll the hair round curlers, secure it with clips or pins, or simply use your fingers. Once dry, you complete the process by dressing the hair with brushes and combs. Hair that has been set is called a **pli**. This term comes from the French *mis-en-pli*, meaning 'put into set'.

As with other techniques, setting produces only a temporary change in hair structure. The pli will be lost as moisture is absorbed by the hair. Various setting aids are available which slow down this process, holding the shape longer.

The client

☆ Prepare your client by removing damp towels and any cut hair. Make sure her clothes are fully covered by the gown.

☆ Communicate with the client about what you are going to do next. Discuss the final effect you are aiming for. Magazines and style manuals may be useful in showing pictures of styles.

☆ Examine the hair again – check the natural direction and movement, the effects of previous perming, and the condition of the hair. Whether a given style is suitable will depend on the texture and condition of the hair.

☆ Agree with your client what you will do. Estimate how long it will take and say if there will be any additional costs.

☆ Analyse the techniques you will need.

☆ Discuss any setting aids you plan to use – your client may have personal preferences.

☆ Assemble the tools you will need, so that they are to hand as you carry out any rolling or pinning.

☆ Advise your client on how to manage the style at home.

Setting aids

When you have towel-dried and combed your client's hair, and before you start work on the pli, you may decide to apply one of a range of **setting aids**. These products help to hold hair in shape, maintain the curls and waves, and thus make the set last longer. They include lotions, sculpting creams, mousses, gels and hair thickeners. Some setting aids also add glaze, glitter, shine or colour to the hair. They contain **resins** or **plastics** (polymers such as **PVP** and **PVA**). These soften the hair, allow shapes to be formed, prevent flyaway effects, and coat the hair with a fine plastic film which slows down the absorption of moisture.

When applying setting aids, remember the following:

☆ If the hair is too wet, the setting aid will become diluted and will be less effective.

☆ If the hair is too dry, it will become sticky and difficult to manage.

☆ Don't apply too much – apart from being wasteful, it will make the hair sticky.

☆ Apply setting aids evenly. Massage or comb them through the hair to make sure each hair is completely covered.

☆ Protect your client's face – chemicals can be irritating to the skin and harmful to the eyes.

☆ Always follow manufacturers' instructions.

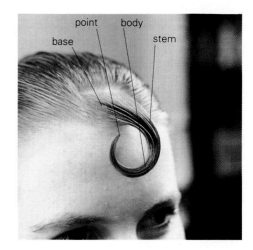

Curl parts

Curling technique

Curls are series of shapes or movements in the hair. They may occur naturally, or be put there by hairdressing – chemically by perming, or physically by setting. Curls add 'bounce' or lift to the hair, and determine the direction in which the hair lies.

Each curl has a **root**, a **stem**, a **body** and a **point**. The **curl base** – the foundation shape produced between parted sections of hair – may be oblong, square, triangular and so on. The shape depends on the size of curl, the stem direction, and the curl type. Different curl types produce different overall effects.

You can choose the shape, size and direction of the individual curls: your choice will affect how satisfying is the finished effect, and how long it lasts. The type of curl you choose depends on the style you're aiming for – a high, lifted

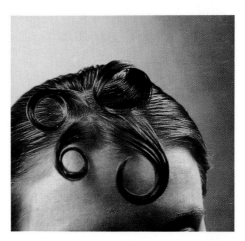

Curl types

Curl bases

Tip

If you're not sure which size of roller is best, use smaller ones – if necessary you can brush out too tightly curled hair later. Loosely curled hair will drop more easily, so you may not achieve the style you were aiming for.

Roller setting

movement needs a raised curl stem; a low, smooth shape needs a flat curl. You may need to use a combination of curl types and curling methods to achieve the desired style – for example, you might lift the hair on top of the head using large rollers, but keep the sides flatter using pincurls. Think about this when designing the pli.

Rollering

There are various sizes and shapes of **roller**. In using rollers you need to decide on the size and shape, how you will curl the hair onto them, and the position in which you will attach them to the base.

☆ Small rollers produce tight curls, giving hair more movement. Large rollers produce loose curls, making hair wavy rather than curly.

☆ Rollers pinned on or above their bases, such that the roots are upright, produce more volume than rollers placed below their bases.

☆ The direction of the hair wound round the rollers will affect the final style – do you want the hair to flick upwards or turn under?

Health and safety

Don't position metal clips or pins on the scalp itself – they will get hot when you dry the hair, and may burn the skin.

Never allow a pin to pierce the skin – watch what you are doing!

Method

1 Begin at the point from which the curled hair is to flow, at a place that is comfortable for the client and convenient to work from.

2 Section the hair to avoid unwanted divisions after setting and drying. Use a tailcomb with which you can divide and control the hair easily.

3 As you work, make sure that any fine, wispy hair is included on the roller. Don't overstretch the hair – this might cause the hair to break or become limp.

4 If you are using pins to secure the rollers, make sure you don't pierce the client's scalp, or disturb hair that has already been wound.

5 Cleanly comb a section of hair – no longer or wider than the roller size being used – straight out from the head.

6 Place the hair points centrally onto the roller. Use both hands to retain the hair section angle and keep the hair points in position.

7 As you turn the roller, 'lock' the hair points against the body of the roller. Then wind down the hair and roller evenly. Don't move the hair from side to side when winding: if you do, the hair will slip out.

8 Place the wound roller centrally onto the sectioned base to achieve the full height effect. Secure the wound roller by pinning through it to prevent unwinding.

Common faults

☆ If you don't secure the wound roller carefully on its base

Roller setting

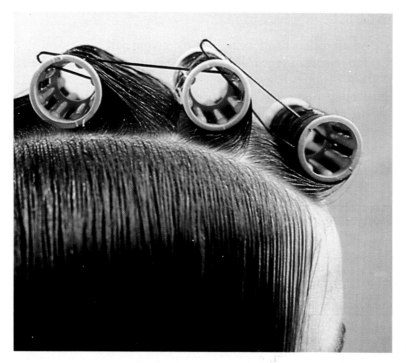

ACTIVITY

Practise setting a circle of curls. This is good in achieving control of stem directions.

Securing rollers

Pinning rollers

ACTIVITY

Practise setting one row of curls with stems to the left, the next with stems to the right, and the third with stems to the left. Dry in position, then brush the hair and blend the curls. You should have achieved a wave shape.

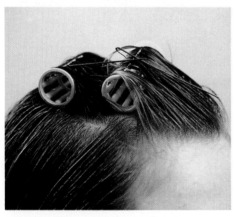

Dragging rollers

you may get a dragged or flat effect, without the volume you had intended.

☆ If the hair sections are too big or too small, you will find it difficult to blend the curls when dressing.

☆ Don't allow roller pins to scratch the skin – it is better to pass them through another roller.

☆ Longer hair requires a large roller, unless very tight effects are required. Large rollers in short hair make control difficult and the effects produced are weak.

☆ Dragging hair from either side of the roller produces divisions which will not dress out easily.

☆ If you bend back the hair points you may cause 'fish-hooks'.

☆ Twisting hair as you roll it will distort the movement of the hairstyle.

☆ Working untidily can lead to sloppy rollering, which in turn causes dressing problems and distorts the movement directions of the final style.

Pincurling

Pincurling is the technique of winding hair into a series of curls which are pinned in place while drying. The two most common types of curl produced in this way are the barrelspring and the clockspring.

☆ The **barrelspring curl** has an open centre and produces a soft effect. When formed, each loop is the same size as the previous one. It produces an even wave shape and may be used for **reverse curling**, which forms waves in modern hairstyles. In this, one row of pincurls lies in one direction, the next in the opposite direction. When dry and dressed, this produces a wave shape.

☆ The **clockspring curl** has a closed centre and produces a tight, springy effect. When formed each loop is slightly smaller than the previous one. It produces an uneven wave shape throughout its length. It can be suitable for hair that is difficult to hold in place, but is not commonly used in modern styling.

Method

The following method of curling can be used for tight or loose, big or small, even and uneven shapes.

1 Neatly section the hair and comb cleanly through it. (The section size is determined by the effect required.)
2 Hold the hair in the direction it is to lie after drying and dressing.
3 Hold the hair, at mid length, in one hand, using the thumb and forefinger, with the thumb uppermost. Using the thumb and finger of the other hand, with the thumb underneath, hold the hair a little way down from the hair points.
4 Turn the second hand to form the first curl loop. The hand should turn almost completely round at the wrist.
5 On completion of the first loop, transfer the hair to the finger and thumb of the other hand.
6 Form a series of loops until the curl base is reached. The last loop is formed by turning the curl body into the curl base. The rounded curl body should snugly fit into the curl base.
7 Secure the curl without disturbing the curl's position on its base. Use clips or pins.

This curling method can be used to produce barrelspring or clockspring curls. The curl loops may be formed either larger or smaller, as required. It can be used whether you are right- or left-handed.

Common faults

☆ Tangled hair is difficult to control – comb the hair well before you start.
☆ If the base size is too large, curling will be difficult, particularly if the hair is short.
☆ If you hold the curl stem in one direction but place it in another you will cause the curl to lift.
☆ If you don't turn your hand sufficiently you will find it difficult to form loops.

Barrelspring curl

Clockspring curl

Stand-up pincurls

Curl variations

Roller, stand-up and barrel pincurls are similarly formed. Each has its stem directed up from the head, which produces height and fullness.

☆ The **stand-up pincurl** is formed on an oblong base – longer than it is wide – and has an open centre and a lifted base. These curls produce high, soft, casual, loose shapes. Their main advantage is individual direction and shape.

☆ **Roller curls** are similar to stand-up curls but do not have the individual shape and movement produced by separate curls. The main difference between these curls is the tension used, and their size.

☆ The **barrel pincurl** is formed on a smaller base than that used for rollering. Variation in stem direction produces interesting shapes. The curl is formed from its points, or held in the centre and the points placed onto the base. A clip retains the lifted base and curl position. Barrel pincurls are normally wider than stand-up pincurls, and narrower than roller curls.

Roller curls

Curl body directions

A flat curl may be either clockwise or counter-clockwise. The body of a clockwise curl moves to the right, like the hands of a clock. The counter-clockwise curl moves in the opposite direction. Roller and stand-up pincurls are formed with their stems directed up from the head.

Make sure that you place the hair carefully to get the curls going in the right direction for the style you have chosen.

Reverse curls

Using alternate rows of clockwise and counter-clockwise barrelspring curls, you can create a wave shape. Double rows of reverse curls – two rows clockwise, then two rows counter-

Barrel pincurl

hair curled like this . . .   . . . combs out to give waves

Curl body directions

Reverse curls

clockwise – produce larger waves. Wave size is determined by the hair length and the curl size, and by the use of single or double rows.

ACTIVITY

Using three separate blocks, form, dry and dress three different curl types. Look carefully at the different effects and consider how you might use each kind of curl in your designs for setting.

Health and safety

Never place clips or pins in your mouth – this is unhygienic and dangerous.

Never place tailcombs in your pockets – they may pierce the body when you bend over.

Never work on a wet, slippery floor.

Always use clean, sterile tools, towels and equipment, to avoid cross-infection.

Drying a pli

The pli is usually dried using a hood dryer, carefully lowered to cover the set head of hair.

1 Make sure the client is comfortable.
2 Set the dryer to a temperature that suits the client. Most dryers have thermostatic controls, but it is a good idea to check with the client from time to time. Fine hair should be dried at lower temperatures.
3 Drying will take about 20–30 minutes. The time will depend on the thickness of the hair: the thicker the hair, the longer the drying time. The dryer may have an automatic timer which reminds you when the time is up.
4 Allow the hair to cool fully before removing pins, clips and so on. If you unwind the hair while it is still warm and soft the shape will soon drop.

Steam setting

The **steam set** relies on the setting of clean, dry hair, with moisture supplied by a steamer.

1 Wash and dry the hair.
2 Place the dry hair into the pli.
3 Steam the hair for three minutes.
4 Place the hair under a dryer for 5–10 minutes, depending on the length of the hair.
5 Allow the hair to cool, then dress it.

This type of set produces a quick shape; the hair is shiny and easy to dress. It takes about half an hour for long hair.

Successful curling

Learning to curl, like other practical techniques, requires patience and practice. It is necessary to experiment, preferably on practice blocks. Try combing, sectioning, sub-dividing smaller hair sections, handling different hair textures, and practising the sequence of movements required to form the curl.

When you are fairly competent, transfer your skills to 'live' models. In a way, this is like starting again. Dealing with the model, and coping with different hair textures, hair lengths and style requirements, creates further opportunities for you to explore techniques of curling.

Reasons for poor results

☆ Wet hair stretches more than dry hair. If the hair is too dry the curl spring will be reduced.

☆ Hot hair is soft. If you start to dress it before it has cooled, spring and shape will be lost.

☆ To form a movement you need to make several similar curls. If you use too few the shape becomes skimped.

☆ If hair is not free of grease and other materials before setting, the shape will be loose and lank.

☆ If you don't dry the hair sufficiently after setting, the shape soon falls.

☆ The larger the curl, the looser the effects. Large rollers placed in short hair produce straight effects.

☆ Frizzy ends may be produced by fish-hooking or overstretching.

☆ Stem direction determines hair movement. If the directions are varied by too much dressing, control becomes difficult.

Finger waving

Finger waving is a technique of moulding wet hair into 'S' shaped movements using the hands, the fingers, and a comb. It is sometimes called **water waving** or **water setting**, as the result resembles waves in the sea. In **horizontal waving** the waves are from side to side; in **vertical waving** they are up and down.

The technique was most popular before rollers were widely available – you can see the effect in the flat, waved hair of early movie stars. Nowadays hairstyles are generally fuller, but finger waves may be used within the overall style – for example, at the lower part of the back of the head, or at the sides. They usually look better if they are at an angle. As with all styling, the use of these movements depends on the individual client's features and head shape.

Forming the wave

1 Use one finger of one hand to control the hair and to determine the position of the wave. Comb the hair into the

first part of the crest, and continue along the head.

2 Place the second finger immediately below the crest formed, and comb the hair in the opposite direction.

3 Form the second crest similarly, to complete the final wave shape.

The elbow and arm should be held above the hand when it is placed on the head. Only the index finger should touch the head. This gives the required control and pressure. A comb with both widely and closely spaced teeth is the most suitable.

Points to remember

☆ Finger waving is most successful on medium or fine hair that is about 10 cm long. Coarse or lank hair can be difficult.

☆ Setting lotion, gel, mousse or emulsion will be needed to hold the waves.

☆ Keep your forearm level with or slightly higher than the wrist, to control the hair and your hand during waving.

☆ Hold the comb upright and don't use too much pressure when combing, to avoid tearing the scalp.

☆ Keep the waves the same size and depth – about 3 cm (the tips of two fingers) between crests is usually best.

☆ For vertical waving, use strips about 5 cm wide.

☆ For short hair, make shallow rather than deep waves.

☆ Pinching or forcing the crests will distort the waves. Correct control and angling will produce the best waves.

☆ Positioning is important – comb the hair to make it lie evenly, and return it to this position after each wave movement is complete.

☆ Keep the hair wet (but not dripping) during waving. If you find that it is drying out, dampen it while you work and apply more setting lotion if necessary.

☆ Dry the completed shape under a hood dryer, if possible. This helps to prevent the movements from being disturbed.

Waving all of the hair

1 Begin the waving about 75 mm from the front hairline, at the parting. The parting should ideally be placed midway above the eyebrow. Start with the larger side of the hair.

2 Place the finger at right angles to the parting, with the crest curved round to the front.

3 If there is to be no parting, begin at the hairline on one side.

Dressing the waves

The waved head of hair is not usually brushed. It should be disturbed as little as possible.

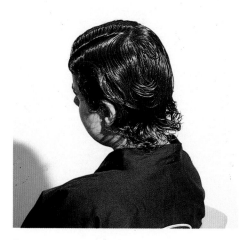

Finger-waving: first crest

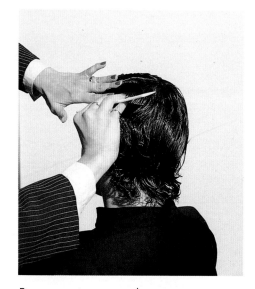

Finger-waving: second crest

Finger-waving: whole head

ACTIVITY

Finger wave different parts of a block or head, and dry the hair in position. Assess the wave shape formed: better waves remain in one position, poor ones drop.

ACTIVITY

On a practice block set the section with the rollers so that it is over-directed. On another block set the top section with rollers on their bases. On a third block set the rollers below sections. Dry and dress all three. Note the shape and the hair direction produced in each.

1 Place the coarse end of the comb between the two lowest crests and comb through to the ends. Support and hold the crests and hair above the combing, to prevent dragging. A slight pushing and moulding action with the hand produces full, soft wave shapes.

2 Repeat this, starting between the next higher crests.

3 Complete the dressing with the fine end of the comb.

Dressing technique

After all the planning and preparation, dressing is the process of adding the finishing touches to well-conditioned, cut and set hair. Setting gives movement to hair in the form of curls or waves. **Dressing** blends and binds these movements into an overall flowing shape, the style you set out to achieve. It produces an overall form that flows, lightening the head and face and removing dull, flat or odd shapes. The completed shape is called a **dressing**, **coiffure** or **hair-do**. It is this that the client takes away from the salon – ideally, a correct and satisfying interpretation of what was required.

Dressing uses brushing and combing techniques, and dressing aids such as hairspray to keep the hair in place. If you have planned the pli carefully and set the hair accordingly, only minimum dressing will be needed.

Dressing in progress (*below*), and completed (*below right*)

Brushing

Brushing blends the waves or curls, removes the partings left at the curl bases during rollering, and gets rid of any stiffness caused by setting aids.

1 One way of achieving the finished dressing is with a brush

and your hand. The thicker the hair, the stiffer the brush bristles need to be. Choose a brush that will flow through the hair comfortably.

2 Apply the brush to the hair ends. Use firm but gentle strokes.
3 Work up the head, starting from the back of the neck.
4 Brush through the waves or curls you have set, gradually moulding the hair into shape.
5 As you brush, pat the hair with your hand to guide the hair into shape. Remember, though, that overdressing and overhandling can ruin the set.

The technique of **double brushing** uses two brushes, applied one after the other in a rolling action. You may prefer to use a brush and comb.

Dressing with a brush

Backbrushing

Backbrushing is a technique used to give more height and volume to hair. By brushing backwards from the points to the roots, you roughen the cuticle of the hair. Hairs will now tangle slightly and bind together to hold a fuller shape. The amount of hair backbrushed determines the fullness of the finished style.

Tapered hair is well suited to backbrushing: the short hairs in the sections backbrushed add bulk easily. Clubbed hair, on the other hand, does not respond to backbrushing as it is all of one length. Tapered hair, with shorter lengths distributed throughout, is more easily pushed back by brushing. Most textures of hair can be backbrushed; because it adds bulk, the technique is especially useful with fine hair.

Method

1 Hold a section of hair out from the head. For maximum lift, hold the section straight out from the head and apply the backbrushing close to the roots.
2 Place the brush on top of the section. With a slight turning action of the brush, slide some of the hairs back towards the scalp. If you brush too strongly you will pull the entire section from your hand. After each stroke, replace the section on the head, in the direction you want it to lie.
3 Check the surface of the section. In the final style the underlying tangling should not be visible.
4 You may need to backbrush only a small amount of hair – it depends how much volume you want to add.
5 Offer your client guidance about how to achieve the same effect at home, and about how to remove backdressing without tearing or breaking the hair.

Backbrushing

Backcombing

The technique of **backcombing** is similar to that of backbrushing. Here a comb rather than a brush is used to turn shorter hairs in a section, giving support and volume to dressed hair. The backdressing is applied deeper in the hair, right down at the roots, so this technique can add more volume than can backbrushing.

Backcombing

Method

1 Hold a section of hair out from the head. Use different angles with different sections.
2 Place the fine end of the dressing comb underneath the section, near the roots. Don't push it too far in. Gently turn it, and push it back towards the head.
3 Repeat this movement of the comb along the length of the section, moving away from the roots and towards the points.
4 Push the backcombed section out of your way, and comb another section. Continue until you have achieved the desired height or fullness.
5 Finish the dressing by positioning the hair with your fingers. Smooth the hair with the wide end of the comb.

Teasing

After brushing the hair and backdressing it if necessary, you may need to place small areas of hair individually. This is called **teasing**.

It is important at this stage not to disturb the rest of the dressing. Use your fingertips and a pin, the end of a tailcomb, or a wide-toothed Afro comb to lift the hair carefully into position, to finish the balance, or to cover an exposed area.

Simple dressing

Hair does not always need backdressing. If the hair has been suitably cut and blow-styled it may already have sufficient shape and bulk. After setting, tonging or hot brushing, for example, this kind of dressing may be quite adequate:

1 Brush the hair firmly, starting at the nape. Gradually work up the head until you reach the front.
2 As you brush, move freely – first *against* the direction of the set, then in the intended direction.
3 Having blended the set in this way, distribute the hair using a comb or brush. Follow the movements of the hair. Lightly stroke the hair with your hand as you position it. Gently push the hair from the head to achieve any extra height.

Tip

Backcombing is applied to the *underside* of a hair section. Don't let the comb penetrate too deeply (towards the surface of the section), or the final dressing will drag the backcombing out and lose the effect.

ACTIVITY

Practise differing amounts of backdressing. Notice how backcombing produces firmer and higher effects than backbrushing.

Tip

Angle your hands so that the palms don't touch the head, and don't pat the hair too much – you could easily undo the effect of the earlier dressing.

Overdressing

One of the commonest faults in dressing is **overdressing** – doing too much. You need to plan the whole dressing from the outset, and watch what you are doing so that you recognise when you have done enough. Don't fiddle with the hair: look for the overall shape, balance and movements.

Mirrors

As you work, use mirrors throughout to check what you are doing. If you spend too long concentrating on one area you will lose track of the overall shape. Step back from time to time and look at the shapes and movements you are producing. This will save time-wasting alterations later.

At the end, hold a hand mirror at an angle so that your client can see the finished effect from behind and from the side.

Long hair

Long hair needs particular consideration, but is not difficult to manage. If it is in good condition and has been well cut it will hang naturally. Flowing styles can be finished with a hand dryer and a brush.

Because long hair is heavy, it is important to centralise the weight. This will help it to stay in place. You can secure it in position using pins, grips, rubber bands, combs or ribbons.

When the bulk of the hair is in place, you may dress lengths by plaiting. If you do use plaits, angle them carefully so that you keep the weight well distributed. Take care not to disturb the *base* of the secured hair – you need this to remain firm.

Pleating

A **pleat**, or **French roll**, is a fold of hair, commonly worn on the back of the head. It is most suitable for long hair, but can be achieved even with shorter lengths. The pleat is one way of dressing long hair to make it appear to be shorter.

Method

1 Brush the hair as a whole. If the pleat is to be placed to the left or right of the centre back, brush the hair initially in the direction required. Secure the top crown hair, placing it out of the way. The side hair may be dressed separately, or dressed in with the back hair.

2 Before placing the pleat, make sure the head is in an upright position. Forward movements of the head will then tighten, rather than loosen, the pleat. (If the pleat is placed when the head is too far forward it will loosen as the head becomes erect.) Backdressing may be used to give added fullness.

3 Place one hand on the head, at the angle at which the pleat is to lie. Secure the hair firmly, using grips.

4 Brush the hair, and place it in the palm of one hand. Grasp and support the hair bulk. Direct the hair ends towards the

Dressing a pleat

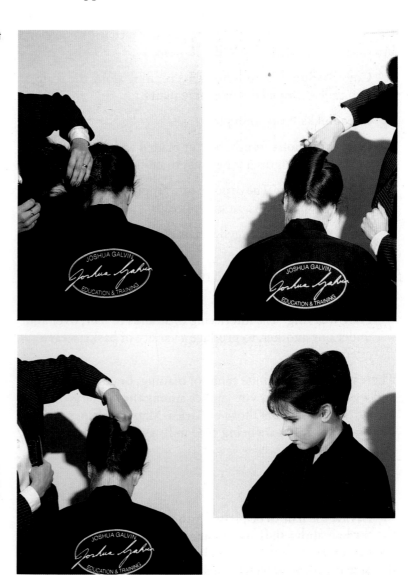

head. At the same time, move the hand up to the crown, thereby spreading the hair.

5 You can now remove the hand from the top of the head: with this hand, position the pleat. Secure the pleat with pins and grips. Put these at the edges, where they are not obvious.

6 When the pleat is secure, dress the sides and top. The front or crown hair may be used to cover the top part of the pleat; the sides may be waved back, curled, draped, or put in ringlets.

Plaiting

Plaiting, or **braiding**, is achieved by intertwining sections of hair. It can be an attractive way of dressing long hair. A variety of sizes and shapes is possible. The three-stem plait is the one most commonly used, but other, multi-stem plaits may be used. Plaited or unplaited hair offers a wide range of dressings. Basket-weave shapes have become popular recently. You can interlace coloured materials, if you wish.

☆ **Cornrowing** Continuous plaits running along the scalp, also called **scalp plaits** or **ethnic plaits**.

☆ **Dreadlocks** Long thin plaits.

☆ **Hair extensions** Synthetic hair plaited and added to the natural hair lengths, by heating, to imitate dreadlocks.

☆ **Hair threading** The process of wrapping plaited, or unplaited, hair with coloured threads.

☆ **Hair twists** Oiled or gelled hair twisted together to form tufts.

☆ **Hair wrapping** Coloured ribbon wrapping the hair, or plaiting with ribbons.

☆ **Hair weaving** The interlacing of strands of hair, over and under one another, to produce a variety of basketweave effects.

There is an almost infinite range of plaiting, braiding, twisting and weaving effects, as you can see among the ethnic groups of the world, particularly those of Africa. Many dressings of international origin are being used in British and European fashions.

Three-stem plaits

1 Divide the hair to be plaited into three equal sections. Hold the hair above the hands, using your fingers to separate the sections.

2 Starting from either left or right, place the outside section

Woven hair, on a block

> ### Health and safety
> Avoid pulling the stems too tightly, particularly at the hairlines. Repeated plaiting, and plaiting left for long periods, can cause traction baldness and hair breakage.

Head-hugging plait

Head-hugging plait when complete

over the centre one. Repeat this from the other side. (Alternatively, place the outside stems *under*, rather than *over*, the central one.)

3 Continue intertwining the outside sections of hair over the centre ones until you reach the ends.

4 Secure the ends with ribbon, thread, or a bow.

Head-hugging patterns

1 Comb the front and top hair together at the crown. Divide it into three equal stems.

2 Starting from the left or right, cross an outside stem over the centre stem. Repeat this action, crossing the opposite stem over the centre stem.

3 With the little finger, take in a further section of hair, about half the thickness of the initial stems. Add it to an outside stem.

4 Cross this thickened stem over the centre one. Repeat this, too, from the other outside stem.

5 Continue in this way, adding hair to each of the outside stems before crossing them over the centre stem.

6 When there is no more hair to be added, continue to plait to the hair ends. Secure the plaits.

Four-stem plaits

1 Divide the hair to be plaited into four equal stems.

2 Begin to plait by crossing the left-hand of the two centre stems *over* the other centre stem.

3 Now cross the outside right stem *over* the next stem.

4 Then cross the outside left stem *under* the next one.

5 Repeat each of these stages until you reach the hair ends.

Six-stem plaits

1 Divide the hair into six equal stems. Form these into two groups of three stems.

2 Pass the outside right stem *over* the next two stems.

3 From the left, pass the outside stem *under* two stems, and *over* one.

4 Repeat this until you reach the hair ends.

Four-stem plait

The more stems you plait, the more help you will need in handling them. A large variety of multi-stem plaits may be formed: try them out! The hair must, of course, be long enough to plait. Control is easier if you oil, or dampen, the hair. Some tension is required, but it should be evenly distributed throughout the plait length.

Ornamentation

Ornaments can be used to enhance and complete hair dressings – combs, ribbons, jewels, grips and slides can all be used; as can flowers, feathers, glitterdust, coloured sprays, beads and sequins.

Added hairpieces – also known as **postiche** – can be an attractive means of ornamentation. Apart from covering injuries or scars, bald patches and other hair defects, they can be decorative and interesting. The means of securing hairpieces vary: most are attached by combs, grips or pins. For a complete change of dressing, styled **wigs** can be used. To see the range of postiche available, refer to wigmaking textbooks or manufacturers' brochures.

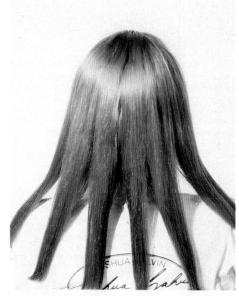

Six-stem plait: starting

Dressing and finishing aids

Hairsprays

Hairsprays contain a variety of chemicals with different functions. These may be dissolved in water or in alcohol. Sprays may contain a **polyvinyl pyrrolidone**, or **PVP**, which helps to reduce the absorption of water from the atmosphere. They may include **plasticisers**, which make the hair more flexible; **cetrimide**, which helps in conditioning the hair and minimising static electricity; or **silicones**, which add sheen to the hair. Finally, they may contain colouring, perfume, or preservatives.

Six-stem plait in progress

Health and safety

Some aerosol sprays contain CFCs (chlorofluorocarbons). These are the propellants which force the spray out of the can. It is now known that CFCs damage the ozone layer in the upper atmosphere. Sunlight contains ultraviolet (UV) light, which can be harmful to the skin: the ozone layer protects us by absorbing most of this UV light.

CFCs are gradually being replaced by less harmful chemicals. Make sure that the hairsprays you use do not contain CFCs.

To achieve a fine spray and an even distribution, hold the can upright, about 30 cm from the hair. (If you hold it closer you will wet the hair and loosen the set: sticky beads will form, and the hair will hang in strands. If you spray from too far away, most of it will miss the hair.) For a firm hold, spray into the roots. For a lighter hold, sweep your hand across the hair. You can always add a little more, but you can't remove it if you've applied too much.

Andrew Collinge, for TRESemmé

Hair ornamentation

Other dressing aids

As you comb or brush hair, especially when it has just been dried, the friction produces **static electricity**. The hairs each carry a very small *positive* charge, causing them to fly away from each other. The brush or comb carries a very small *negative* charge, which attracts the positively-charged hair. You can reduce the amount of static by lightly touching the hair with your hand, which earths it. There are also dressing aids which may help: these include control creams, oils, gels and mousses.

These aids may be used for other reasons, too – to add gloss, to hold the hair, or to make combing smoother. **Emollients** or **moisturisers**, such as lanolin and olive oil, reduce water loss; **humectants**, such as glycerine, absorb moisture.

Dressing aids come in various forms, including aerosols. Some are applied to wet hair and others to dry hair – always check the manufacturers' instructions before using them.

How to succeed

Checklist

In preparing for assessments on style setting, the following list may be useful. Check that you have covered and fully understood these items:

☐ determining the techniques you should use to achieve the required style;

☐ applying these techniques;

☐ practising the different types of curls;

☐ agreeing where finger waves may be used;

□ discussing the amount of dressing, if any, to be used;
□ applying rollers and understanding the effects achievable;
□ comparing the differences between rollering, pincurling, etc.;
□ understanding the effects of setting on hair structure;
□ applying relevant safety factors and precautions.

Self-check quiz

Oral and written questions are used to test your knowledge and understanding. Try the following:

1 What determines hair direction when curling?
  (a) the points
  (b) the body
  (c) the stem
  (d) the size

2 Reverse curls produce:
  (a) frizz
  (b) fish-hooks
  (c) waves
  (d) curls

3 The effect of setting curls is:
  (a) permanent
  (b) natural
  (c) temporary
  (d) chemical

Oral test

With the help of a colleague, give spoken answers to the following questions.

1 Describe the different curl effects.
2 What are the differences between rollering and pincurling?
3 Why use different curl types?
4 How does setting differ from blow-styling?
5 Name some common setting faults.

Written test

Answer the following questions in writing.

1 With reference to the curling of hair:
  (a) describe the different curl parts;
  (b) state how curls are formed and secured;
  (c) name three different kinds of curl, and their effects;
  (d) describe the effects of curls on hair structure;
  (e) list the precautions to be taken.

2 Describe the following aspects of curling:
   (a) the different techniques;
   (b) the main differences between these techniques;
   (c) the tools that may be used;
   (d) the materials that may be used;
   (e) some examples of how curls may be used effectively in a pli.

Andrew Collinge, for TRESemmé

Perming

Perming – principles

Perming – also known as **permanent waving** or **curling** – is a technique for making straight hair curly. Some methods use warmth, but the most popular techniques, called **cold perming** (or **CPW**), do not. Unlike the curls produced by setting and blow-styling, the curls produced by perming really are permanent: the hair does not straighten out later when it absorbs water from the atmosphere. However, hair grows, and new hair takes its natural form. So the waves and curls produced by perming gradually get further and further from the scalp as the hair grows. To keep the style, sooner or later the hair will need to be permed again.

Because perming really does make a permanent change to the hair, you cannot easily correct mistakes (as you can with blow-styling, for example). The process also involves various chemicals. It is therefore important that you make sure you understand what you are doing.

How perming works

The structure of keratin

As discussed in Unit 2, hair contains a protein called **keratin**. Keratin is made from many amino acids which are joined together in long chains called **polypeptides**. Within each chain, and between neighbouring chains, there are **cross-links**. These determine the three-dimensional structure of the keratin.

There are three kinds of cross-link: the weakest are hydrogen bonds; next come salt linkages, which are somewhat stronger; and strongest of all are disulphide bridges. Each **disulphide bridge** is a strong bond between two sulphur atoms. Within each polypeptide chain there are amino acids called **cysteine**. Part of the cysteine is a group containing a

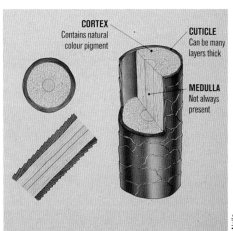

CORTEX
Contains natural colour pigment

CUTICLE
Can be many layers thick

MEDULLA
Not always present

Wella

Cross-section of hair

Effect of perming on hair structure

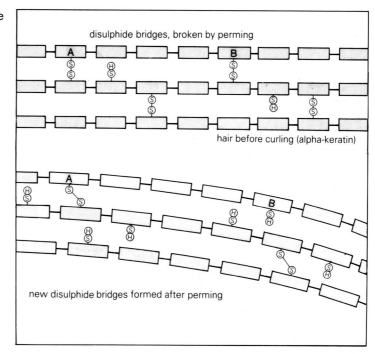

disulphide bridges, broken by perming

hair before curling (alpha-keratin)

new disulphide bridges formed after perming

sulphur atom and a hydrogen atom. If a cysteine in one chain lies next to a cysteine in an adjacent chain, the hydrogen may be lost and the sulphur atoms may bond together, forming a different amino acid, called **cystine**. These disulphide bridges give the hair its strength. The process of perming breaks these disulphide bonds and allows different ones to form.

Only about 20 per cent of the disulphide bonds need to be broken during a perm. If too many are broken, the hair will be damaged. You need to keep a check on the progress of the perm, and stop it at the right time. You do this by rinsing away the perm lotion and **normalising** (or **neutralising**) the hair.

Changing the bonds

The hair is first wound onto some kind of **former**, such as a **curler** or **rod**. Then you apply perm lotion to the hair, causing it to swell. The lotion flows under the cuticle and into the cortex. Here it reacts with the keratin, breaking some of the cross-links within and between the polypeptide chains. This softens the hair, allowing it to take up the shape of the former. You then rinse away the perm lotion, normalise the hair, and allow it to harden in its new, curlier shape.

This process is often described using terms from chemistry. The first part – softening the hair by breaking some of the cross-links – is called **reduction**. The disulphide bridges are split by the addition of hydrogen from the perm lotion. (The chemical in the perm lotion that supplies the hydrogen is called

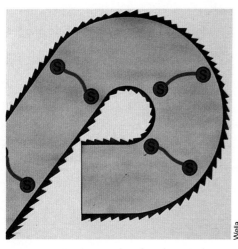

Disulphide bridges

Wella

a **reducing agent**.) The keratin is now stretched: it is beta-keratin.

The last part of the process – hardening the hair by making new cross-links – is called **oxidation**. New disulphide bridges form, and the hydrogen that was added is lost again. The hydrogen reacts with the oxygen in the normaliser to form water. (The chemical in the normaliser that supplies the oxygen is called an **oxidising agent** or **oxidant**). The keratin is now in a new, unstretched form: it is alpha-keratin again.

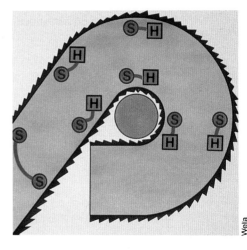

Reduction: breaking existing disulphide bridges

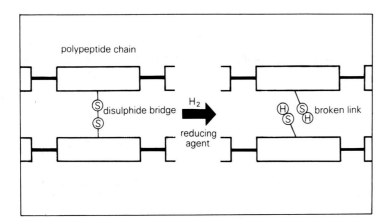

Reducing agents

In the past, most cold perming lotions were alkaline, but these tend to roughen the cuticle. Newer lotions are acidic instead, and these are becoming popular.

Perm lotions often contain **ammonium thioglycollate**. This is environmentally damaging, and new perm solutions use other chemicals.

Oxidising agents

Hydrogen peroxide is the best-known oxidant. Others include sodium perborate, sodium percarbonate, sodium bromate, and potassium bromate.

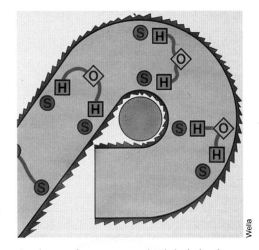

Oxidation: forming new disulphide bridges

Planning the perm

The client

For the client a perm is a major step – she will have to live with the result for several months. She may not understand the range of perms available: she will need you to explain what is involved in each and to help her decide which is the most suitable.

☆ There are several cold perms designed to curl straight hair.

See the brochures produced by manufacturers.

☆ Acid perms are popular because their effects are gentle. Strongly alkaline perms are too harsh: new forms are being developed.
☆ Not all perms contain ammonium thioglycollate: 'non-thio' perms tend to be gentler in their action.

Discuss your client's requirements. Find out what she is expecting from a perm, and determine whether this is the best solution.

☆ Consider the style and cut, your client's age, lifestyle, etc.
☆ Examine the hair and scalp closely. If there are signs of inflammation, disease, and cut or grazed skin, do *not* carry out a perm. If there is excessive grease or a coating of chemicals or lacquer you will need to wash these out first. Previously treated hair will need special consideration (discussed later in this unit).
☆ Analyse the hair texture. Carry out the necessary tests to select the correct perm lotion.
☆ Always read manufacturers' instructions carefully.
☆ Determine the types of curl needed to achieve the chosen style.
☆ If this is a regular client, refer to her record card for details of previous work done on her hair.
☆ Advise your client of the time and costs involved. Summarise what has been decided, to be sure there is no misunderstanding.
☆ Minimise combing and brushing, to avoid scratching the scalp before the perm.

Examination

It is important to make sure you choose the most suitable perm lotion, the correct processing time, and the right type of curl for the chosen style. Consider the following factors.

☆ **Hair texture** For hair of medium texture, use perm lotion of normal strength. Fine hair curls more easily and requires weaker lotion; coarse hair is harder to wave and requires stronger lotion.

☆ **Porosity** The porosity of the hair determines how quickly the perm lotion is absorbed. Porous hair in poor condition is likely to process more quickly than hair with a resistant, smooth cuticle (see Units 2 and 3).

☆ **History of hair processing** 'Virgin' hair – hair that has not previously been treated with chemicals – is likely to be more resistant to perming than hair that has been treated. It will require a stronger lotion and possibly a longer processing time.

☆ **Length and density of hair** Long, heavy hair requires more perming than short hair because the hair's weight will pull on the curls. Short, fine hair may become too tightly curled if given the normal processing time.

☆ **Style** Does the style you have chosen require firm curls or soft, loose waves? Do you simply wish to add body and bounce?

☆ **Size of rod, curler or other former** Larger rods produce larger curls or waves; smaller rods produce tighter curls. Longer hair generally requires larger rods. If you use very small rods in fine, easy-to-perm hair, the hair may frizz; if you use rods that are too large you may not add enough curl. To check, make a test curl before you start.

☆ **Incompatibility** Perm lotions and other chemicals used on the hair may react with other chemicals that have already been used, for example in home-use products. If the hair appears dull this may indicate the presence of such chemicals. Ask your client what products she uses at home, and test for incompatibility (see below).

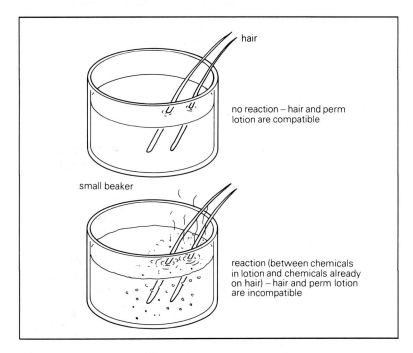

Incompatibility reactions

Tests

☆ **Cleanliness** Check that the hair is clean. Dirt or grease will block the action of the perm, and the results may be straight rather than curly.

☆ **Elasticity** Stretch a hair between your fingers. If it breaks easily the cortex may be damaged, and perming could be harmful.

☆ **Porosity** Rub the hair between your fingertips to feel how rough or smooth it is. Rougher hair is likely to be more porous, and will therefore process more quickly.

☆ **Incompatibility** Protect your hands by wearing gloves. Place a small cutting of hair in a mixture of hydrogen peroxide and ammonium hydroxide. Watch for signs of bubbling, heating or discoloration: these indicate that the hair already contains incompatible chemicals. The hair should not be permed: nor should it be tinted or bleached. Perming might discolour or break the hair, and the skin might be burnt.

☆ **Test curl** Wind, process and normalise one or more small sections of hair. The results will be a guide to the optimum rod size, the processing time, and the strength of lotion to be used. Remember, though, that the hair will not all be of the same porosity.

☆ **Processing** Unwind – and then rewind – rods during processing, to see how the curl is developing. If the salon is very hot or cold this will affect the progress of the perm: heat will accelerate it, cold will slow it down. When you have achieved the 'S' shape you want, stop the perm by rinsing and then normalising the hair.

Perm rods, curlers and formers

Perming technique

Perming is a straightforward procedure – the more organised you are, the simpler and more successful it will be. Once you have consulted your client and made the necessary tests, you are ready to start.

Preparation

1 Protect your client as necessary with a gown and towels.
2 Shampoo the hair to remove grease or dirt which would otherwise block the action of the perm lotion.
3 Towel-dry the hair. (Excess water would dilute the perm lotion, but if the hair is too dry the perm lotion won't spread thoroughly through the hair.)
4 Some perm lotions contain chemicals to treat porosity. If you are going to use a pre-perm lotion, apply it now. Make sure you have read the instructions carefully – too much pre-perm lotion may block the action of the perm itself.
5 Prepare your trolley. You will need:
   ☐ rods, curlers or formers of the chosen sizes;
   ☐ end papers, for use while winding;
   ☐ a tailcomb and clips, for sectioning and dividing;

□ cottonwool strips, to protect your client;
□ gloves, to protect your hands;
□ perm lotion and a suitable normaliser (read the instructions carefully);
□ a water spray, to keep the hair damp;
□ a plastic cap and a timer for the processing stage.
6 Check that your client's skin and clothing are adequately protected.

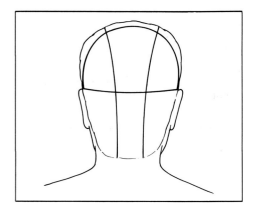
Sectioning

Sectioning

The first operation is to divide the hair into **sections**. This makes the hair tidier and easier to control. Done properly, sectioning makes the rest of the process simpler and quicker. If it's not done well, though, you will have to re-section the hair during the perm, and this may spoil the overall result.

Cold perm sectioning

1 Following shampooing and towel-drying, comb the hair to remove any tangles.
2 Make sure you have the tools you will need, including a curler, to check the section size.
3 Now divide the hair into nine sections, as follows. Use clips to secure the hair as you work.
   □ Divide the hair from ear to ear, to give front hair and back hair.
   □ Divide the back hair into lower, nape hair and upper, top back hair.
   □ Divide the front hair, approximately above mid-eyebrow, to give a middle and two sides.
   □ Divide the top section along the same lines, to give a middle and two sides.
   □ Divide the nape section likewise, to give a middle and two sides.

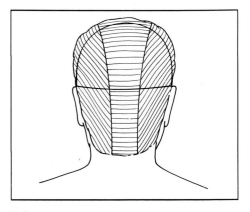
Sub-sectioning

This is not the only way of sectioning a head of hair, but it is a good one to start with. When you have mastered this method you can try others.

Sectioning may seem cumbersome at first. Keep practising: it will get easier, and your movements will become quicker and neater. Don't be surprised if it all seems different again when you section a live head. It takes time to get used to the different lengths, textures and conditions of hair – and unlike a practice block, clients don't always stay still!

Winding

Winding is the process of placing sectioned hair onto rods, curlers or formers. There are various winding techniques, designed to produce different effects, but the method is

ACTIVITY

On a block, and later a model, practise sectioning techniques until you can work quickly and efficiently. Practise with the hair wet and with it dry. Your first attempts on a live head may be disappointing, until you are used to the client moving around and the different textures, lengths and conditions of hair.

Tip
Wear gloves from the beginning – it is inconvenient having to put them on later.

Winding: taking a hair section

Winding the section onto the curler

Winding: securing the section

basically the same in each case. In modern cold perming systems you need to wind the hair firmly and evenly, but without stretching the hair or leaving it in tension.

First practise winding wet hair on a block. It should be dampened with water rather than perm lotion, as this gives you more time. When you can wind a block in 40–60 minutes, move on to a live model. When you can do this in 20–30 minutes, you can try 'live perming' with perm lotion.

Method

1. Divide off a section of hair, of a length and thickness to match the curler being used.
2. Comb the hair firmly, directly away from the head. Keep the hair together, so that it doesn't slip.
3. Place the hair points at the centre of the curler. Make sure the hair isn't bunched at one side and loose at the other.
4. Hold the hair directly away from the head. If you let the hair slope downwards, the curler won't sit centrally on the base section: hair will overlap, and the curler will rest on the skin.
5. Before winding, make sure the curler is at an angle suited to the part of the head against which it will rest when wound.
6. Hold the hair points with the finger and thumb of one hand. The thumb should be uppermost.
7. Direct the hair points round and under the curler. Turn your wrist to achieve this. The aim is lock the points under the curler and against the main body of hair – if they don't lock, they may become buckled or fish-hooked. Don't turn the thumb too far round or the hair will be pushed away from the curler and won't lock the points.
8. After making the first turn of the curler, pass it to the other hand to make the next turn. The hands need to be in complete control: uncontrolled movement, or rocking from side to side, may cause the ends to slip, the hair to bunch, or the firmness to slacken.
9. After two or three turns the points will be securely locked. Wind the curler down to the head. Keep the curler level – if it wobbles from side to side, the hair may slip off or the result may look uneven.
10. At the end, the curler should be in the centre of the section. If it isn't, unwind it and start again.
11. Secure the curler. Don't let the rubber fastener press into the hair – it might damage it.

Winding techniques

There are various winding techniques, used to produce varied effects. The following are the most commonly used.

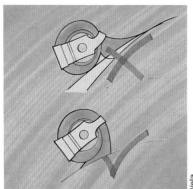

Winding: depth of section (*far left*) and width of section (*left*)

☆ **Spiral winding** The hair is wound from roots to points, around a variety of sticks, shapers, hair moulders, or curlers of one shape or another. Triangular and square shapers have been used. The effects produced are mainly in the lengths of the hair, the root ends being less affected. This is probably the oldest form of winding. It is most effective, and most practical, with long hair.

☆ **Croquignole winding** This starts at the hair points and works down to the roots. This technique has been commonly used for a number of years in cold perming. It is best used where the hair curl needs to be strongest at the points. (The term 'croquignole' comes from the old wigmaker.)

☆ **Directional winding** Winding the hair in the direction in which it is to be finally worn. This technique is suitable for enhancing well-cut shapes. The hair can be wound in any direction required, and the technique is ideal for shorter hairstyles.

☆ **Staggered winding** or **brick winding** Placing the wound curlers in the fashion of brickwork. By staggering the partings of the curlers, you avoid obvious gaps in the hair. It is suitable for short hairstyles.

☆ **Weave winding** Dividing the normal-size section into two and weaving the hair. A large curler is used to wind the upper sub-section, and a smaller one is used for the lower sub-section. This produces two different curl sizes, giving volume without tight curls. Alternatively, one sub-section is wound and the other left unwound. With short hair this produces spiky effects.

☆ **Double winding** Winding a section of hair halfway down on a large curler, then placing a smaller curler underneath and winding both curlers down to the head. This produces a varied curl effect.

Spiral winding

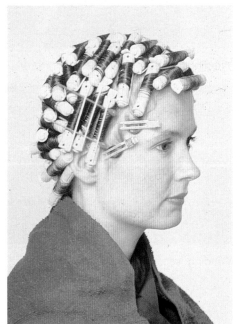

Directional winding

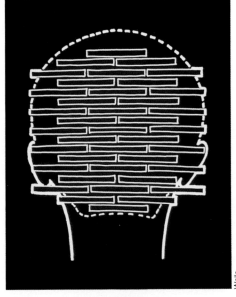

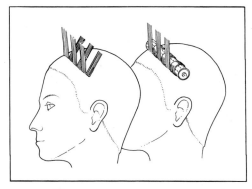

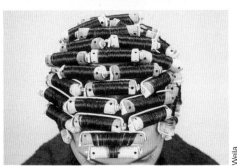

Staggered or brick winding

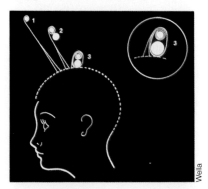

Double or twin winding

Weave winding

☆ **Piggyback winding** Winding with a small and a large curler. The normal-size section is wound from the middle onto a large curler, down to the head. The ends are then wound from the points onto a smaller curler, which is placed on top of the large curler. This produces softly-waved roots and curly points. Alternatively this technique can be used to produce root movement only by not winding the point ends.

☆ **Stack winding** This is used where fullness of long hair is

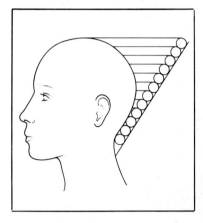 

Stack winding

required, with little curl movement on top – it is ideal for bobbed hair lengths. The sections are wound close to the head in the lower parts; the upper sections are part wound only, at the points. This allows the curlers to stack one upon another.

To appreciate the effects of different techniques of winding you need to experiment with them. Many professionals are continually trying out new approaches, sometimes with exciting results.

Winding aids

☆ The **tailcomb** is useful in directing small pieces of hair onto the curler. Don't let the tail pass around the curler, as this causes unevenness and hair may slip out of the wound section.

☆ **End papers** or **wraps** are specially made winding aids. They ensure control of the hair when it is wound. Fold them neatly over the hair points – never bundle them. The wrap overlaps the hair points and prevents fish-hooking. For smaller or shorter sections of hair, half an end wrap is sufficient – a full one would cause unevenness. Other types of tissue may absorb the perm lotion and interfere with processing: these are best avoided.

☆ **Crêpe hair** is useful for holding the hair points when winding: it allows enough grip and prevents ends slipping. As with end papers, only a little should be used – too much causes the hair to bunch together.

> **ACTIVITY**
>
> Try out different curlers, rods and winding shapes. Note the varied effects they produce.
>
> Practise the different curler positions for perming. Try these out on blocks or models to appreciate the differences.

ACTIVITY

On a practice block of sample hair cuttings, experiment with the effects produced by different faulty windings. This will help you to recognise and to avoid these effects.

☆ Many kinds of **curler** are suitable for cold perm winding. Plastic, wood, bone and china are amongst the materials used. Different colours are used to indicate size. The greater the diameter, or the fatter the curler, the bigger the wave or curl produced. The smallest curlers are used for short nape hair, or for producing tight curls. Most curlers are of smaller diameter at the centre: this enables the thinner hair points to fill the concave part evenly and neatly as the hair is wound. This is particularly useful with tapered hair. Clubbed hair should be evenly spread across the centre of the curler.

Processing

Perm lotion may be applied before winding (**pre-damping**) or when winding is complete (**post-damping**). Follow the manufacturer's instructions. Post-damping is perhaps more convenient: you can wind the hair without wearing gloves, and the time taken in winding doesn't affect the overall processing time. Processing begins as soon as the perm lotion is in contact with the hair.

Applying the perm lotion

Most perm lotions come in an applicator bottle, ready to use. Others may need to be applied from a bowl, using cottonwool, a sponge or a brush. Read the instructions carefully before applying.

☆ Underlying hair is usually more resistant to perming. Apply lotion to these areas first.
☆ Keep lotion away from the scalp. Apply it to the section, about 12 mm from the roots.
☆ Don't overload the applicator, and apply the lotion gently. You will be less likely then to splash your client.
☆ If you do splash the skin, quickly rinse the lotion away with water.

Processing time

The time needed for processing is critical. Processing time is affected by the hair texture and condition, the salon temperature and whether heat is applied, the size and number of curlers used, and the type of winding used.

☆ **Hair texture and condition** Fine hair processes more quickly than coarse hair, and dry hair than greasy hair. Hair that has been processed previously will perm faster than 'virgin' hair.

☆ **Temperature** A warm salon cuts down processing time; in a cold salon it will take longer. Even a draught will affect the time. Usually the heat from the head itself is enough to activate cold perming systems. Wrap your client's head with plastic tissue or a cap to keep in the heat. Don't wrap the hair in towels: these would absorb the lotion and slow down the processing.

Some perm lotions require additional heat, from lamps or dryers. Don't apply heat unless the manufacturer's instructions tell you to – you might damage both the hair and the scalp. And don't apply heat unless the hair is wrapped – the heat could evaporate the lotion, or make the processing happen too fast.

☆ **Curlers** Processing will be quicker with a lot of small sections on small curlers than with large sections on large curlers. (The large sections will also give looser results.)

☆ **Winding** The type of winding used, and the tension applied, also affect processing time. A firmer winding processes faster than a slack winding – indeed, if the winding is too slack it will not process at all. Hair wound too tightly may break, close to the scalp. The optimum is a firm winding without tension.

Health and safety

Don't pack curlers with dry cottonwool. This would absorb the perm lotion; it would also put it in direct contact with the skin, causing irritation.

Mop up any surplus lotion on the skin, then use a barrier cream or place a water-dampened band of cottonwool to protect the skin. Don't let barrier cream get onto the hair, as this would spoil the process.

Testing curls during processing

As processing time is so critical, you need to use a timer. You also need to check the perm at intervals to see how it's progressing. If you used the pre-damping technique, check the first and last curlers that you wound. If you applied the lotion after winding, check curlers from the front, sides, crown and nape.

☆ Unwind the hair from a curler. Is the 'S' shape produced correct for the size of curler used?
☆ If the curl is too loose, rewind the hair and allow more processing time. (However, if the test curl is too loose because the curler was too large, extra processing time will damage the hair and won't make the curl tighter.)
☆ If the curl is correct, stop the processing by rinsing.

Tip
During processing, don't leave your client while you do something else. You might lose track of time or forget to check the curls. Also, your client might become anxious.

Rinsing and normalising

When processing is complete, leave the curlers in place while you rinse away the perm lotion. Use tepid water (not hot). Direct the spray head onto and between the rollers for several minutes to make sure all the lotion is removed. Long hair will require more rinsing than shorter hair.

After rinsing, blot the hair with towels and cottonwool to remove excess water. The hair is now ready for normalising – see Unit 10.

This is the point at which to apply rinses or conditioners. Before doing so, however, check the manufacturer's instructions.

After the perm

☆ Check the results of perming.
  ☐ Has the scalp been irritated by the perm lotion?
  ☐ Is the hair in good condition?
  ☐ Is the curl even?
☆ Dry the hair into style.
  ☐ Depending on the effect you want, you may now use finger-drying, hood-drying or blow-drying.
  ☐ Treat the hair gently – if you are too firm the perm may relax again.
☆ Advise the client on how to manage the perm at home.
  ☐ The hair should not be shampooed for a day or two.
  ☐ The manufacturer of the perm lotion may have supplied information to be passed to the client.
  ☐ Discuss general hair care with your client.
☆ Clean all tools thoroughly so that they are ready for the next client.
☆ Complete the client's record card. Note details of the type of perm, the strength of the lotion, the processing time, the curler sizes and the winding technique. Record any problems you have had. This information will be useful if the hair is permed again.

Perming faults and what to do about them

Fault	Action now	Possible cause	Action in future
The perm is slow to process	Increase warmth but do not dry out; check the winding tension and the number of curlers	Winding is too loose	Wind more firmly or use smaller curlers
		The curlers were too large, or too few were used	Use smaller curlers or more of them

Fault	Action now	Possible cause	Action in future
		The wrong lotion was used	Double-check labels on bottles
		The sections were too large	Take smaller ones
		The salon is too cold	The temperature should be comfortable
		Lotion was absorbed from the hair	Don't leave cottonwool on the hair
		Too little lotion was used	Don't skimp the lotion or miss sections
The scalp is tender, sore or broken	Apply first aid	The curlers were too tight	Don't apply too much tension when winding
		The wound curlers rested on the skin	Curlers should rest on the hair
		Lotion was spilt on the scalp	Keep lotion away from the scalp
		There was cottonwool padding soaked with CPW lotion between the curlers	Renew the cottonwool as necessary, or don't use it
		The hair was pulled too tightly	Don't overstretch it
		The perm was overprocessed	Time perms accurately
There are straight ends or pieces	Re-perm, if the hair condition permits*	The curlers or sections were too large	Take sections no longer or wider than the curler used
		Sections were overlooked	Check that all hair has been wound
		Too few curlers were used	Put curlers closer together
		The winding was too loose	Be a little firmer next time
		Lotion was applied unevenly	Take care to apply it evenly
There are fish-hooks	Remove by trimming the ends	The hair points were not cleanly wound	Comb the hair cleanly
		The hair points were bent or buckled	Place hair sections evenly onto the curlers
		The hair was wrapped unevenly in the end papers	Curl from the hair points
		Winding aids were used incorrectly	Take more care; practise winding

Fault	Action now	Possible cause	Action in future
Hair is broken	Nothing can be done about the broken hair; after discussion with your senior or tutor, condition the remaining hair	The hair was wound too tightly	Wind more loosely next time
		The curlers were secured too tightly	Secure them more loosely
		The curler band cut into the hair base	Keep it away from the hair base
		The hair was overprocessed	Follow the instructions more carefully
		Chemicals in the hair reacted with the lotion	Test for incompatibility beforehand
The hair is straight	Re-perm, if the hair condition permits*	The wrong lotion was used, given this texture	Choose the lotion more carefully
		The hair was underprocessed	Time perms accurately
		The curlers were too large for the hair length	Measure the curlers beforehand
		The normalising was incorrectly done	Follow the instructions more carefully
		Rinsing was inadequate	Rinse more thoroughly
		Conditioners used before perming were still on the hair	Prepare the hair more carefully
		The hair was coated and resistant to the lotion	Check for substances that block the action of perm lotion; shampoo if necessary
The hair is frizzy	Cut the ends to reduce the frizziness	The lotion was too strong, given the hair texture	Assess texture correctly; select suitable lotions; read manufacturers' instructions
		The winding was too tight	Practise and experiment to avoid this
		The curlers were too small	Choose more suitable curlers
		The hair was overprocessed	Time perms accurately
		The normalising was incorrectly done	Follow the instructions more carefully
		There are fish-hooks	Avoid bending hair points when winding
The perm is weak and drops†	Re-perm, if the hair condition permits*	Lotion was applied unevenly	Apply it evenly

Fault	Action now	Possible cause	Action in future
		The normaliser was dilute	Follow the instructions more carefully
		Normalising was poorly done	Be more careful
		The hair was stretched while soft	Handle the hair gently
		The curlers or sections were too large	Use more curlers
Some hair sections are straight	Re-perm, if the hair condition permits*	The curler angle was wrong	Wind correctly
		The curlers were placed incorrectly	Wind correctly
		The curlers were too large	Use smaller curlers
		Sectioning or winding was done carelessly	Practise before perming again
The hair is discoloured	Tone the hair to correct this	Metal in the tools or containers reacted with the lotion	Test for incompatibles beforehand
		Chemicals coating the hair reacted with the lotion	Check for substances that block the action of perm lotion; shampoo if necessary

* Don't re-perm the hair unless its condition is suitable. For example, you should not re-perm if the hair is overprocessed. Conditioning treatments, cutting and careful setting and styling may help. Discuss the problem with your senior or tutor.

† Before attempting to correct this fault, make sure that the hair is not overprocessed. Dampen the hair to see how much perm lotion there is.

How to succeed

Checklist

In preparing for assessments on permanent waving, the following list may be helpful. Check that you have covered and fully understood these items:

- ☐ determining the style and agreeing this with the client;
- ☐ assessing the hair type and condition, noting whether it is virgin or treated, and whether long, medium or short;
- ☐ selecting the type of perm lotion;
- ☐ adequately preparing the client and her hair;
- ☐ sectioning the hair appropriately;
- ☐ determining the type of winding to use;
- ☐ matching techniques to the style effects required;
- ☐ processing the perm and testing it regularly;

☐ applying normaliser as required;

☐ conditioning and finishing the perm into style.

Self-check quiz

Oral and written questions are used to test your knowledge and understanding. Try the following:

1 The strongest link within and between keratin chains is:
(a) a protein
(b) a hydrogen bond
(c) a disulphide bridge
(d) a salt bridge

2 A reduction process involves the addition of:
(a) hydrogen
(b) sulphur
(c) oxygen
(d) nitrogen

3 The normalising process involves the formation of:
(a) carbon
(b) water
(c) hydrogen peroxide
(d) polypeptides

Oral test

With the help of a friend, give spoken answers to the following:

1 Why is it necessary to section the hair for perming?
2 Describe the chemical process of cold perming.
3 Name the different stages of cold perming.
4 What is the oxidation process?
5 Describe the structure of keratin.

Written test

Answer the following questions in writing:

1 Describe cold perming, including:
(a) its effects on the hair structure;
(b) the sectioning and winding processes;
(c) the perm processing and normalising stages;
(d) precautions to be taken and tests to be made;
(e) the correction of faults that might arise.

2 State the effects of perming on hair structure. Also:
(a) describe what happens to keratin;
(b) describe the reduction process;
(c) describe the normalising process;
(d) list oxidants that may be used;
(e) list precautions to be taken.

Goldwell

Colouring, bleaching and toning

Colouring – principles

We are surrounded by colour. Look around the salon – at clothing, make-up, nail varnish, accessories, pictures, decor and packaging. Hair too can be colourful. Its colour can contribute to the overall style as much as its cut and finish. Throughout the ages people have sought to change the colour of their hair to keep up with fashion, for social or religious reasons, to enhance their appearance, and to feel better about the way they looked.

It is hard to define colour – words like 'chestnut' and 'blonde' describe them but are not sufficiently precise. This unit introduces the International Colour Chart and examines some basic facts about colour. It also discusses the techniques of colouring – bleaching, tinting and toning, and less permanent ways of altering hair colour. Products have improved considerably over the years: their quality and effects are now of a high standard. You need to have equally high standards in their application and use.

Seeing colour

When you see an object, what you are actually seeing is light reflected from it. White light is really a mixture of many colours – that is why sunlight reflected by falling rain can produce a rainbow. A white object *reflects* most of the white light that falls upon it; a black object *absorbs* most of the light falling on it. A red object reflects the red light, and absorbs everything else.

Hair colour depends chiefly on the **pigments** in the hair, which absorb some of the light and reflect the rest. The colour is also affected by the light in which it is seen, and (to a lesser extent) by the colours of clothes worn with it.

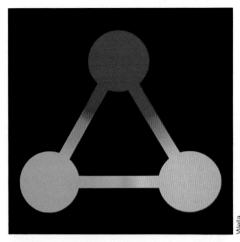

The colour triangle

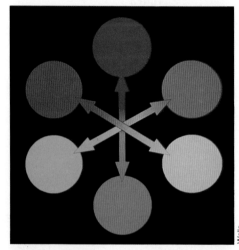

The colour circle

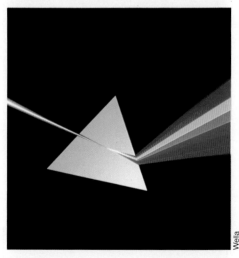

The colour spectrum from visible light

Mixing colours

The pigments in *paints* give three **primary colours** – red, blue and yellow. Pairs of these give the **secondary colours** – purple, green and orange. The various other colours are made from different proportions of the primary colours. White and black can be added to vary the **tone** of the colour.

The primary colours in *light* are different – red, green and blue. (These are the three colours used in a colour television.) The secondary colours are yellow, cyan and magenta. The many colours in 'white' light can be separated by a glass prism or by rain: we see the **spectrum** of colour from white light as red–orange–yellow–green–blue–indigo–violet.

Hair colour

As discussed in Unit 2, the **natural** or **base colour** of hair depends on pigments within the cortex of the hair. **Melanin** colours the hair black or brown; **pheomelanin** colours it red or yellow. The colour you see therefore depends on the amounts and proportions of these pigments. If the hair contains no pigment at all, it is white or blonde. (The pale yellow in this case is due to the keratin, not to pigment.) Children who start with blonde hair may get darker later as more melanin is produced.

Some people never have any pigment in their hair, a condition known as **albinism**. Such people usually have no colour in the eyes or skin either. Sometimes there is just a little colour present: this condition is called **partial albinism**.

With age, or following stress, pigment may no longer be produced. Hairs already on the head will be unaffected, new ones will be white. The proportion of white hairs among the coloured ones gradually increases, and the hair appears to go 'grey' – however, there aren't actually any grey hairs. 'Greyness' is often expressed as a percentage. For example, '50% white' means that half the hairs on the head are white, and half are their original colour.

Describing hair colour

☆ The **depth** of colour refers to how light or dark the colour is: this depends on the intensity of the pigments within the hair.

☆ The **tone** is the colour that you see – the combination of pigments that give the overall colour. 'Warm' shades, such as gold or auburn, have more pheomelanin; 'cool' shades, such as ash, cendre, matt or drab, have less.

The **International Colour Chart** (**ICC**) offers a way of defining hair colours systematically. Even here, though, charts may vary between manufacturers. Take note of the way each manufacturer describes the different colours.

Shades of colour are divided and numbered, with black (1) at one end of the scale and lightest blonde (10) at the other. *Tones* of other colours (0.01–0.9) are combined with these, producing a huge variety of colours. Charts are usually arranged with shades in rows down the side and tones in columns across the top. To use them, first identify the shade of your client's hair: that row of the chart then shows the colours you could produce with that hair. For example, if your client has light brown hair (shade 5) and you tint with an orange tone (0.4), the result should be a light warm brown (5.4). The possibilities are almost endless, as these examples indicate:

☆ to produce ash shades, add blue;
☆ to produce matt shades, add green;
☆ to produce gold shades, add yellow;
☆ to produce warm shades, add red;
☆ to produce purple or violet shades, add mixtures of red and blue.

Hair colourings

Hair colourings, or **colourants**, may be grouped according to how long they remain on the hair:

☆ temporary colourings are applied as hair lotions, creams, mousses, and the like;
☆ semi-permanent colourings are applied as hair creams and rinses;
☆ permanent colourings are applied as tints.

There are many different colouring products, developed from a variety of materials including vegetable extracts and minerals.

Vegetable colourings

These are made from the flowers, stems or barks of various plants.

☆ **Henna**, or **Lawsone**, is made from the powdered leaves of the Egyptian privet. It is used to add red colour to hair.

☆ **Camomile**, made from the flower of the camomile plant, has a yellow pigment. It is used to add yellow to light hair, thereby brightening the hair. It colours the surface only.

☆ **Indigo**, made from the leaves of the indigo plant, gives a blue-black colour. When mixed with henna in different proportions it produces a variety of shades.

☆ **Walnut**, made from the outer shell coverings, yields a yellow-brown dye. It is a surface, non-penetrating colourant.

DEPTHS	
1/0	Blue Black
2/0	Black
3/0	Dark Brown
4/0	Medium Brown
5/0	Light Brown
6/0	Dark Blonde
7/0	Medium Blonde
8/0	Light Blonde
9/0	Very Light Blonde/Lightest Blonde
10/0	Extra Light Blonde/Pastel Blonde

Wella

TONES	
/0	Natural
/1	Ash
/2	Cool Ash
/3	Honey Gold
/4	Red Gold
/5	Purple
/6	Violet
/7	Brunette
/8	Pearl Ash
/9	Soft Ash

Wella

Wella

Health and safety

Compound henna is incompatible with modern colouring and perming materials. Don't confuse it with vegetable henna.

Two shade charts

Health and safety

Metallic dyes are incompatible with modern hairdressing materials. Always make tests before using bleach, oxidation tints or cold perm normalisers with them.

Health and safety

Dyes or tints such as these may cause a skin reaction. Carry out a skin test before applying them.

ACTIVITY

In your styling book, record the different colour products available. Collect examples from journals and magazines.

☆ **Quassia**, made from the bark of a tree, is often used with camomile to produce a useful colourant which brightens hair.

Other substances, including sage, sumach, oak bark, cubear and logwood, have been used for their varied shades and effects.

Vegetable and mineral colourings

These consist of a mixture of vegetable extracts and mineral substances. One of the commonest was **compound henna** – vegetable henna mixed with metallic salts. This surface colourant is no longer used in the salon.

Mineral colourings

These are divided into two groups: metallic dyes and aniline derivatives.

Metallic dyes are surface-coating colourings. They are variously known as reduction, metallic, sulphide and progressive dyes. They are not commonly used in the salon, but are occasionally found in 'hair colour restorers'.

Aniline derivatives come from the distillation of coal tar, as do many chemicals used in cosmetics and medicines. These synthetic organic dyes, often known as **'para' dyes**, include para-phenylenediamine and para-toluenediamine. These dyes penetrate the cortex of the hair as small molecules. They are then treated with an oxidising agent such as hydrogen peroxide. This makes them combine into larger molecules which remain 'trapped' in the cortex: shampooing cannot wash them out.

You can use these aniline dyes both to lighten the melanin and to tint the hair at the same time.

Using hydrogen peroxide

Hydrogen peroxide is one of the most commonly used oxidising agents. It can be mixed with cream or with liquid tints. The mixture appears colourless at first, but darkens on exposure.

With a modern tint and hydrogen peroxide, the mixture first penetrates the cuticle. In the cortex, the natural colour pigment is bleached, and the colourant is oxidised. The tint becomes 'locked' within the cortex. (Note that peroxide is needed even when you are making the hair *darker* – not to lighten the natural pigment, but to fix the tint in the cortex.)

To lighten the natural hair colour ('colour up') two or three shades, use a higher strength of hydrogen peroxide. To take the natural colour 'down' to a darker shade ('colour down'), use a lower strength. The percentage strength to use is determined by the manufacturers' instructions, the colour of the hair to be lightened or darkened, and the hair's porosity. (See the table of hydrogen peroxide dilutions on pages 163–4.)

Pre-lightening is necessary when the natural colour is to be changed to a very light shade. Mixtures of hydrogen peroxide and ammonium hydroxide (or other bleaching agents) may be used. Modern colourings lighten several shades, but cannot by themselves lighten to the very light tones.

Pre-softening is a technique used on resistant hair. Dilute hydrogen peroxide and ammonium hydroxide are applied, not to lighten the colour but to soften the cuticle. This makes it easier later for the colourant to penetrate the hair.

Tinting aids

The activation of colouring processes can be aided by the use of steamers, accelerators or rollerballs. The applied heat causes the hair to swell and the cuticle to lift. This makes it easier for the colourant to enter the cortex, and may halve the processing time.

Steamers, accelerators and rollerballs allow tint applications to be made on hair regardless of the length, even though the hair may vary in its porosity between the roots and the points. The heat distribution allows even processing throughout the hair length. However, colour application must not be delayed or the result may be uneven.

Choosing colour

The choice of colour depends on the following factors:

☆ **The client's requirements** Think about your client's age, lifestyle, job, fashion and dress sense, and the colours she wears (both clothing and make-up). Younger clients may want bright colours or black. Older clients may wish to disguise the fact that their hair is going grey. In general, choose colours from a natural range that blend with the natural colour – avoid bright, harsh colours that contrast with it.

☆ **The natural hair colour** The client's base shade depends on the amounts and relative proportions of melanin and pheomelanin. With darker hair it may be necessary to lighten the natural colour before colouring the hair.

☆ **The client's skin colour** In nature the colour of the skin tends to blend with the colour of the hair. You are altering that balance, so be careful. A deep red tint would clash with a ruddy complexion, for example; blonde, cool tints would look odd on oriental and warm, dark skins. The amount of melanin in skin increases when the skin is

Colour to suit the client's lifestyle

> **Tip**
> If in doubt, always choose the lighter shade – it is easy to add extra colour if required, but more difficult to remove unwanted colour.

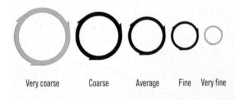

Very coarse   Coarse   Average   Fine   Very fine

Hair textures

exposed to sunlight, so the skin darkens – this is what we see as a **tan**. (The production of extra melanin is the body's defence against the ultraviolet light from the sun. Too much UV light may cause skin problems, including cancer.)

☆ **The hair texture** The thickness or fineness of the hair affects the absorption of colouring chemicals. In general, fine hair will tint more rapidly than coarse hair.

☆ **The condition and porosity of the hair** Porous hair will absorb tints quickly, and porosity depends on the general condition of the hair. Hair with a smooth cuticle absorbs less tint. Uneven colour may result.

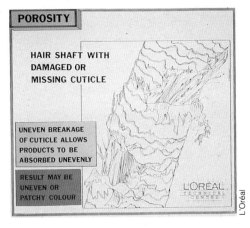

Porosity and its causes

☆ **The colouring product used** Tests on the hair will indicate which products may be used. This will affect the range of colours available to this particular client. For example, tests may show that it is correct to use a light, temporary colouring, but there is no point in using it on dark hair – it wouldn't show.

☆ **The shade of colour sought** This too may influence the suitability of various products. A white-haired client, for instance, may want to have a slight tone added. In this case a temporary or semi-permanent colouring might be best, in a colour such as silver, pewter, blue or violet. Lighter colourings will be preferable to heavy, darker ones; they will match the skin colour better.

The client

Your client may ask many questions about colour. What colour would be best? How can that colour be achieved? How long will it last? How much will it cost? How will it affect the hair? Is the hair suitable? You need to be ready with answers to such questions on all aspects of hair colouring before you start work on your client's hair.

☆ Discuss the client's ideas about colouring, considering the style and how colour may enhance it. Are there factors that might influence the choice of colour, such as the client's lifestyle?
☆ Examine the hair for previous colouring, perming and other chemical treatments. What is its natural colour?
☆ Analyse the state of the hair and consider the effects of colouring treatments on it. Determine the hair's condition, porosity and elasticity.
☆ Refer to the client's record card, if available.
☆ Decide what sort of colouring to carry out, and agree with your client on the product you will use. Refer to a colour chart to make sure you really are agreed about the colour.
☆ Advise your client how long the process will take and how much it will cost.
☆ Carefully read the manufacturer's instructions for each product you are going to use.
☆ Prepare your client with a gown and other coverings. Make sure all clothing is protected.
☆ Keep brushing and combing to a minimum – if you scratch the scalp, you will make it sensitive to the chemicals you will be using.

Tests

Strong chemicals are involved in hair colouring and bleaching – if misused, these could damage the hair or skin. The following are tests you should carry out, most before you start, one during processing.

Most permanent colourings contain chemicals that irritate certain skin types. This is usually stated on the label. Always test the skin 24–48 hours before applying such colourings, so that you know how the skin is likely to react. Don't assume that a product is safe just because it has been used on this client before – a skin reaction may develop even after regular use.

☆ **Skin test** A test to find out whether the client's skin reacts to chemicals in the permanent colourings you are going to use (see below). It is also known as the **predisposition test**,

> **Tip**
>
> Some clients are sensitive to chemicals in tints – the tints may cause an allergic reaction on first use. Other clients become allergic later. You must make a skin test *each time* you use a tint.
>
> Ask whether the client is allergic to anything else, such as washing-up liquid, make-up or certain foods. If she is, she is more likely to react to tinting products.

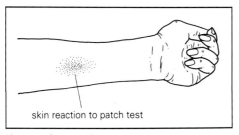

skin reaction to patch test

Skin test for an allergic reaction

patch test, or **Sabouraud–Rousseau test.** The method is as follows:

1 Mix a little of the tint to be used with the correct amount and strength of hydrogen peroxide.
2 Clean an area of skin about 8 mm square, behind the ear or in the arm fold. Use spirit on cottonwool to remove the grease from the skin.
3 Apply a little of the tint mixture to the skin. Allow it to dry.
4 Cover the tint patch with collodion, which protects it.
5 Ask your client to report any discomfort or irritation that occurs in the next 24–48 hours. Arrange to see the client at the end of this time so that you can check for signs of reaction.
6 If there is a **positive response** – *any* skin reaction, such as inflammation, soreness, swelling, irritation or discomfort – do not use this colouring treatment. *Never* ignore the result of a skin test. If a skin test showed a reaction and you carried on anyway, there might be a much more serious reaction: this might affect the whole body, and it might for example lead to dermatitis. If there is a **negative response** – no reaction – you can carry out the treatment proposed.

☆ **Colour test** A test for the suitability of a chosen colour, the amount of processing that will be required, and the final colour that will result. Apply the tint or bleaching products you propose to use to a cutting of the client's hair.

☆ **Porosity** A test to indicate how fast chemicals will be absorbed. Rub the hair between your fingertips – is the cuticle smooth or rough? The rougher the cuticle, the more porous it is, and the faster it will absorb chemicals.

☆ **Elasticity** A test for hair strength. Pull a hair between your fingers. Does it stretch and spring back? If the hair breaks easily it may be that the cortex is damaged, in which case chemical processing might cause it to break.

☆ **Incompatibility** A test for chemicals already on the hair. Use gloves to protect your hands. Place a sample of hair in a mixture of hydrogen peroxide and ammonium hydroxide. If the mixture bubbles, heats up or discolours, you should *not* apply a tint – to do so would cause severe damage.

☆ **Strand test** A test during processing, to check progress – see page 150. If the colour is uneven or insufficient, further processing or more tint is required.

Colouring technique

Temporary hair colourings

Temporary colourings remain on the hair only until washed off. They do not penetrate the hair cuticle, nor do they directly affect the natural colour. They merely coat the surface of the hair. Some colourings may nevertheless be absorbed if the hair is porous and its condition poor. Temporary colourings are supplied as setting lotions and creams, coloured hairsprays and lacquers, hair colour crayons and paints, glitterdust, mousses, and gels. Many contain **'azo' dyes**.

There are several advantages to temporary colourings:

☆ the colour effect is only temporary;
☆ a wide range of colours is available;
☆ the colourants are easily removed, by washing;
☆ hair condition is improved;
☆ subtle toning can be applied to grey, white or normal hair;
☆ fashion effects can be used on bleached hair;
☆ no skin test is required.

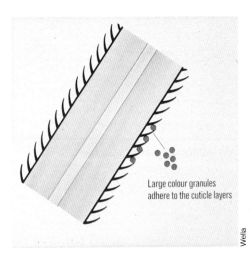

Large colour granules adhere to the cuticle layers

Temporary hair colouring

Types of temporary colouring

☆ **Setting lotions and creams** are popular forms of colouring. The colour is usually carried in a setting agent, which gives 'body' to the hair. No mixing or dilution is required. The colourant is applied with a sponge or brush, or directly from the container. It may be distributed throughout the hair by light frictioning with the fingers. Towel-dry the hair before applying the lotion or cream, to prevent dilution.

☆ **Coloured hair lacquers** are temporary colourings that may be sprayed onto dry, dressed hair. Based on shellac, lacquers coat the hair cuticle, and can be removed by brushing and washing. There is a restricted range.

☆ **Coloured hairsprays** are made in liquid or powder form, and in various colours. They are used on dry, dressed hair. These are based on plastics: they coat the cuticle and are also easily removed by brushing and washing. Some contain metallic colourings – silver and bronze are popular, for example.

☆ **Hair colour crayons and paints** are mainly for theatrical effects. They are particularly useful for highlighting a dressing for the stage or for television.

☆ **Glitterdust** is made from shining, coloured metal dust. When sprinkled on the hair, it produces a twinkling effect.

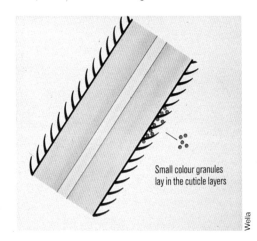

Small colour granules lay in the cuticle layers

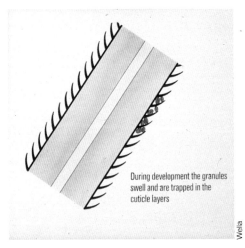

During development the granules swell and are trapped in the cuticle layers

Cosmetic hair colouring

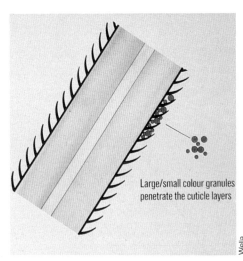

Large/small colour granules penetrate the cuticle layers

Wella

Semi-permanent hair colouring

Gold and silver are commonly used. The effects are temporary and ornamental.

☆ **Coloured mousses and gels** are popular forms of temporary colouring with advantages similar to those of coloured setting lotions. They are able to colour and condition hair, and add extra 'hold'.

Semi-permanent colourings

Semi-permanent colourings are made in various forms and normally require no mixing, unlike some temporary rinses and permanent colourings. However, you should always check the instructions before using any commercial product.

Semi-permanent colouring is deposited in the cuticle and outer cortex. It remains in the hair longer than temporary colourings do. The colouring gradually lifts each time the hair is washed. Some last through six, seven or eight washes. Semi-permanent colourings are not intended to cover a large percentage of white hair, but they nevertheless do so to a greater extent than temporary colourings.

The colour range is varied, but you need to choose carefully. A black rinse on white hair, for instance, will not produce a pleasing result. Timing and development are affected by salon temperature, and by the hair's texture and porosity. Heat and poor hair condition may speed absorption.

Semi-permanent colourings have several advantages:

☆ they are more effective and longer-lasting than temporary colourings;
☆ a larger colour range and choice is available;
☆ root regrowth is less noticeable, as the colour lifts anyway by the time contrasting hair has grown;
☆ natural hair colour is not affected, either directly or chemically;
☆ skin tests are not usually required (but always check the instructions before you start);
☆ foaming agents within the colourants help to prevent colour dripping.

Semi-permanent colourings may be made from nitrodiamines, nitrated aminophenols, and picramic acid. These are collectively known as **'nitro' dyes**. The pigment molecules penetrate the cuticle and enter the cortex, but are gradually removed by subsequent washings.

Preparation

1 Check the scalp for cuts, sores, or any abnormalities that may be aggravated by chemicals in the colouring.
2 Use suitable protective coverings to protect both yourself and your client.
3 Wash the hair with a suitable shampoo, preferably one made for pre-colouring. (Some semi-permanents contain a detergent and require no pre-shampooing.)
4 Remove excess water to prevent colour dilution.
5 Comb through the hair to remove any tangles.

Application

1 Apply the colouring using a sponge, a brush, an applicator bottle, or by pouring it direct from the container, according to the manufacturer's instructions.
2 Apply it evenly, and leave the hair loose to allow free circulation of air. This helps even development. Large hair sections may be taken. (When *tinting*, small sections must be taken.)
3 Do not apply heat without first covering the hair. A plastic cap may be useful, to prevent the colouring drying out, which would adversely affect colour development.
4 Remove any skin stains with spirit or stain remover. Barrier creams help to prevent skin staining.
5 Time the process, following the manufacturer's recommendations.
6 Remove surplus colouring by thorough rinsing, but without further washing.

Permanent colourings

A wide variety of **permanent colourings** is now available. They are used to cover white hair and most natural colours, to produce other natural colours, and fashion and fantasy shades. Modern colourings are made in cream, semi-viscous and liquid forms. Most need to be mixed with hydrogen peroxide: this oxidises the hair's natural pigment and combines the small molecules of synthetic colouring. This process is called **polymerisation**. Without hydrogen peroxide the synthetic colouring would rapidly be lost again.

Tinting is the process whereby the synthetic colouring penetrates the hair cuticle, and is absorbed into the cortex. There it is oxidised and remains permanently fixed. The natural colour is bleached at the same time. Although the colours are permanent, the choice of product, and the rate of hair growth, affect how long the colour lasts. The condition of the hair also affects this: hair with damage to the cuticle (which can be caused by the effects of weather) will lose the colour more rapidly.

Tiny colour granules are mixed with hydrogen peroxide – they pass through the cuticle into the cortex

Wella

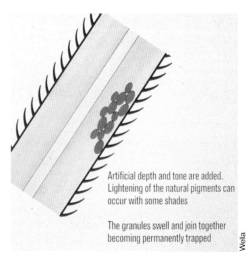

Artificial depth and tone are added. Lightening of the natural pigments can occur with some shades

The granules swell and join together becoming permanently trapped

Wella

Permanent hair colouring

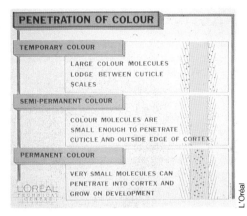

PENETRATION OF COLOUR	
TEMPORARY COLOUR	
LARGE COLOUR MOLECULES LODGE BETWEEN CUTICLE SCALES	
SEMI-PERMANENT COLOUR	
COLOUR MOLECULES ARE SMALL ENOUGH TO PENETRATE CUTICLE AND OUTSIDE EDGE OF CORTEX	
PERMANENT COLOUR	
VERY SMALL MOLECULES CAN PENETRATE INTO CORTEX AND GROW ON DEVELOPMENT	

L'ORÉAL TECHNICAL

L'Oréal

Preparation

Before colouring a client's hair you must make the usual preparations: consulting with the client, agreeing what is to be done, and making the necessary tests (see pages 144–5). Examine the hair and skin thoroughly for signs of poor condition or inflammation. When you carry out the skin test – 24–48 hours before processing – don't forget to take a cutting of the client's hair so that you can make colour tests. Unless you know exactly what products have been used on the hair previously, test for incompatibles such as metallic dyes. The results of these tests will then be available when the client returns for the actual tinting.

Health and safety

Tints contain strong chemicals. Unless you are using the tint as a toner after pre-bleaching, always apply tint to dry, unwashed hair. Shampoo washes away the natural oils which protect the hair and skin from the chemicals in the tint. It also stimulates the skin, bringing blood to the surface and increasing the risk of skin reactions.

Gather together everything you will need:

☆ protective coverings, both for you and your client;
☆ barrier cream to protect the skin around the hairline;
☆ rubber gloves;
☆ glass measures and hydrogen peroxide, for mixing the tint;
☆ a dish and an applicator;
☆ a tailcomb and clips, for sectioning;
☆ cottonwool, to soak up excess tint;
☆ the chosen tint or tints.

Sectioning

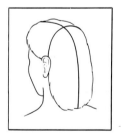
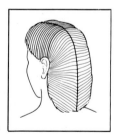

Hair lower down the head, especially hair covered by other hair, is usually darker than that on the top. This is because of the effects of combing and brushing, which make the cuticle more porous, and because outer layers are lightened by sunlight.

Section the hair from the centre of the forehead to the nape, and from ear to ear across the crown. When tinting, take sub-sections about 6 mm wide, starting from the nape.

Mixing the tint

Don't mix the tint until you're ready to start tinting! Once mixed, it needs to be used immediately.

Mix the tint carefully, measuring amounts accurately. If the proportions are wrong, the result may not be as you intended.

Add the peroxide to the tint gradually, to make sure the mixture is smooth.

Application

1 Place the tint bowl near your client, to minimise the risk of dripping tint on her or on the floor.
2 The method of application depends on how runny the tint mixture is. Cream tints are best applied with a brush. Carefully lay the tint onto the sub-section and leave it: don't scrape it off again. With practice you will judge how much to put on. Liquid or semi-liquid tints can be applied with a sponge, an applicator, a dispenser or directly from the bottle.
3 If the tint is thick, work with small sub-sections. The thinner it is, the larger the sub-sections, because it will penetrate more quickly. The applicator brush often gives the best control.
4 Work swiftly and methodically, from the nape upwards.
5 Distribute the tint evenly, covering each sub-section. Too little tint will produce varied colour; too much will be wasteful.

Processing

Time the processing from the point when all of the hair has been treated. Timing must be accurate. Too short a time will cause **underprocessing** – the tinting will be incomplete and the colour won't be as you intended. Too long a time may cause **overprocessing** – the shades produced may be too dark. You may be able to use steamers or accelerators to shorten the processing. Check the manufacturer's instructions.

When you think processing may be complete, carry out a **hair-strand colour test**.

1 Most colouring products require the time recommended by the manufacturer. Check the instructions.
2 Rub a strand of hair lightly with a paper tissue or the back of a comb, to remove the surplus tint.
3 Check whether the colour remaining is evenly distributed throughout the hair's length. If it is even, remove the rest of the tint. If it is uneven, allow processing to continue, if necessary applying more tint.
4 If any of the hair on the head is not being treated, you can compare the evenness of colour in the tinted hair with that in the untinted hair.

Removing surplus tint

Some tints can be removed by adding a little water, lightly massaging the hair, and rinsing. Others may require

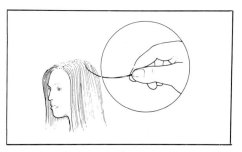

The hair strand colour test

shampooing. Don't ruffle the hair at this stage or it may get tangled.

If there are any **skin stains**, apply a little tint directly to the stain to soften it. Then rinse the skin thoroughly. Don't let the stain remain on the skin for long, as the colour will deepen.

While the hair is wet the colour will look darker. Towel-dry the hair and the true colour will be easier to assess.

Virgin hair

Hair that has not been tinted or otherwise chemically treated before will vary in lightness and porosity along its length. The mid-lengths are usually the most resistant to tinting, and so they take the longest. The hair points are naturally lighter and more porous, because they are the most exposed to wear and weather. The roots are closest to the head, heat from which activates the tint.

For the first tint, therefore, use this special method:

1 Begin by applying tint to the mid-lengths (the main part of the hair).
2 Then apply tint to the hair points (the last 25 mm of the hair tips).
3 Finally, apply tint to the roots (the 12 mm nearest the scalp).

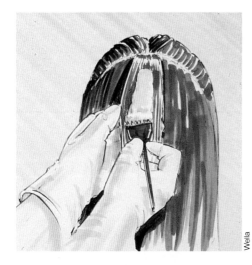

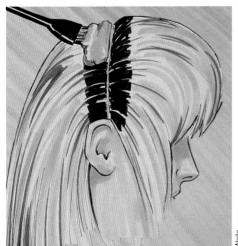

First-time (virgin hair) application

Regrowth tinting

Regrowth tinting is the process of tinting just the hair that has grown since the tint was applied last time. Tint is applied to the root ends only, not to the mid-lengths or points. It is then processed and rinsed in the usual way.

With some tints you can comb the colourant through the rest of the hair after processing. This dilutes the tint and maintains an even colour throughout the hair, correcting any lifting that has occurred.

Tinting lighter or darker

With modern oxidation tints it is possible to lighten or darken the natural hair shade. As usual, you need to plan the final colour, taking into account the starting colour, the texture and condition of the hair, and so on.

To darken the hair, you will need a darker tint and not too much hydrogen peroxide. To lighten it, more peroxide will be needed to oxidise the pigment in the hair. If the client wants the hair lightened by many shades (from black to light blonde, for example), you will need to pre-bleach it.

Regrowth tinting

Resistant hair

Some hair resists tint, usually because the cuticle isn't porous. With experience you will learn to recognise this just by feeling the hair – rough hair is more likely to be porous. Hair is likely to tint easily in certain conditions:

☆ if has recently been permed;
☆ if it usually takes a perm quickly;
☆ if it curls easily and tightly;
☆ if it has previously been coloured;
☆ if it has been bleached;
☆ if it is dry.

It is likely to be resistant:

☆ if it takes perms slowly;
☆ if it soon drops out of curl;
☆ if it has a smooth surface (a tightly-packed cuticle);
☆ if it is greasy or lank;
☆ if it is covered with chemicals or a metallic coating.

White hair is sometimes resistant, but often it is *more* porous than pigmented hair. If there are white patches, tint them last of all, especially if you are using warm shades such as red.

If necessary, pre-soften the hair by applying a diluted mixture of hydrogen peroxide and ammonium hydroxide. This will cause the cuticle to lift, making the hair more porous.

Tip

Don't repeatedly comb *undiluted* tint through the hair after a regrowth tint. This would spoil the final colour and damage the hair.

Competition and fantasy colouring

This involves the application of colourants to produce a variety of special effects. The results may not be natural or suitable for normal wear: some **competition colours** are good examples of wearable colours, others are harsh and garish as a fashion or style requirement. **Fantasy colours** are more extreme, with vivid and startling colour blends.

Lighting plays an important part in colour effects and needs to be considered when planning the overall effect. Lighting has effects in the salon, as well as on competition colourings. Some of these are as follows:

☆ blue light, produced by some types of fluorescent tube, tends to neutralise the warm red effect of hair colour;
☆ yellow light, as from bare electric bulbs, adds warmth to hair colour and tends to neutralise blue or ash effects;
☆ whiter daylight lights show a truer hair colour than artificial light.

Colours planned for special competitions can look completely different if the lighting has not been considered. In the salon the client's colour should be planned to fit the lighting in which the hair is to be seen. For example, a typist working most of the day under a blue fluorescent light will look greenish if the hair is coloured (or left) yellow.

ACTIVITY

You need to be clear about the different kinds of colouring – bleaching, temporary colour, semi-permanent colour, and permanent colour. Make a list of these; then, in each case, say:
☐ which parts of the hair are affected;
☐ the normal processing time;
☐ how long the colour is expected to last;
☐ what are the effects on the hair structure.

Successful colouring

Precautions

Certain precautions need to be taken when using colour or colouring products:

☆ Always carry out a skin test 24–48 hours before tinting. (This is recommended by most manufacturers.)
☆ Make other tests, for hair colour and incompatibles.
☆ Examine the hair and scalp for disease, inflammation, or abnormalities. Avoid adverse skin reactions and the aggravation of existing problems.
☆ Choose colours wisely. Wrong colour applications will undermine your client's confidence.
☆ Check applicators before use. Clean and replace all tools and materials after use. Any remaining tint could discolour light or blonde hair.
☆ Do not try to make temporary colourings do the work of permanent ones. Use products as intended by their manufacturers.
☆ Use reliable products, correctly stored and carefully maintained. Poor-quality products result in loss of time, effort and money – and clients.
☆ Measure quantities accurately – never rely on guesswork.
☆ Avoid the use of metal containers, or hair discoloration may result.
☆ Avoid harsh rubbing and hair ruffling when pre-shampooing or removing colourants.
☆ Protect the hands and skin by using rubber or plastic gloves.
☆ Remove surplus water before tinting, to avoid dilution of colour.
☆ Keep hair colourants away from the eyes. Never use scalp hair colourants on eyebrows or eyelashes: special, non-irritant preparations are made for eyebrows and lashes.
☆ Check the numbers on the tubes or bottles with the numbers on their containers. It is easy to put a tube in the wrong box!
☆ Use correct dilutions of colourants and correct volume strengths of hydrogen peroxide.
☆ Work methodically and efficiently: this will produce confidence in the client, and good results.
☆ Remove stains from clothes immediately, using clean water. If allowed to remain they may become more difficult to remove.

ACTIVITY

Where possible, take colour photographs of successful colourings. Keep them in folders or your styling book.

☆ Ensure that all information is carefully recorded on the client's record card.

Faults and corrections

☆ *Colour is patchy or uneven*:
☐ there was insufficient coverage by the tint;
☐ the tint was poorly applied;
☐ the colour mixing was poor;
☐ the sections were too large;
☐ overlapping occurred, causing colour build-up in parts;
☐ the tint was underprocessed (the full colour did not develop);
☐ a spirit-based setting lotion was used, which has removed some colour.
Correct by spot tinting the light areas.

☆ *Colour is too light*:
☐ there was insufficient colour in the chosen shade;
☐ the peroxide strength was too low to allow full colour development;
☐ the tint was underprocessed;
☐ the hair was in poor condition (too porous to hold colour);
☐ the peroxide strength was too high, causing bleaching and not enough colour to be oxidised.
Correct by reconditioning, colour filling, choosing a darker shade, and checking the peroxide strength.

☆ *Colour fades after two or three shampoos*:
☐ these are the bleaching effects of the sun;
☐ the tint was underprocessed;
☐ the hair has received harsh physical treatment (e.g. brushing, sand);
☐ the hair was in poor condition (too porous).
Correct by reconditioning before the next colour application; process correctly; do not repeatedly comb the colour through.

☆ *Colour is too dark*:
☐ the colour chosen was too dark;
☐ the hair was overprocessed;
☐ the hair was in poor condition (too porous);
☐ the hair was coated by incompatible chemicals.
Correct by using a chemical **hair colour reducer** or **stripper**, as recommended by the manufacturer. Reducers are specially designed to reduce or remove synthetic hair colour.

☆ *Colour is too red*:
☐ the peroxide strength was too high;

☐ if pre-bleached, the wrong neutralising colour was chosen;

☐ colour development was incomplete;

☐ the hair was not bleached light enough.

Correct by applying a matt or green colour to neutralise.

☆ *Hair has discoloured*:

☐ the hair was in poor condition (too porous) and did not hold the colour;

☐ undiluted tint was repeatedly combed through the hair;

☐ the hair may have been coated with incompatible chemicals;

☐ if green, the colour may result from blue ash on a yellow base, or from a metallic salt reaction;

☐ if mauve, the colour may result from reaction with incompatible chemicals.

Correct the green colour with a contrasting colour, but beware of producing dark brown. Correct the mauve colour with a contrasting colour, or remove with special colour reducers.

☆ *Colour coverage is good except for the white hairs*:

☐ the hair was resistant.

Correct by pre-softening, or by using a lighter shade with higher-volume peroxide.

☆ *Hair is resistant to tint generally*:

☐ the cuticle is closely packed;

☐ the tint was underprocessed;

☐ the colour chosen was incorrect;

☐ materials were poorly mixed or poorly applied.

Correct by pre-softening; select the colour carefully; time development correctly; check that you mix and apply the tint properly.

☆ *Scalp irritation or skin reaction has occurred*:

☐ the hair was not cleanly washed – tint was still present;

☐ the peroxide used was too strong;

☐ hair was badly combed and tint poorly applied;

☐ the client is allergic to the tint chemicals.

Correct by giving no treatment other than to wash the hair thoroughly if necessary. Send your client to her doctor. Notify the salon's insurance company.

Bleaching – principles

How bleaching works

A **bleach** is a chemical used to lighten the colour of hair. To be effective, bleach needs a ready supply of oxygen. In hairdressing the most common source of this oxygen is **hydrogen peroxide**, a colourless, oily liquid. In use, peroxide is dissolved in water.

Hydrogen peroxide (H_2O_2) is an **oxidant**: it readily reacts to produce a lot of oxygen. Because it is so reactive, peroxide needs to be stabilised by other chemicals (such as sulphuric acid or phosphoric acid) and stored carefully. To allow the peroxide to work you need to counteract these stabilisers. This is done by mixing it with ammonium hydroxide or (for powder bleaches) sodium acetate or ammonium carbonate. These 'activate' the peroxide.

When you use bleach you mix it with peroxide diluted to the appropriate strength (see below). The bleach now begins to work. The hair swells and the cuticle lifts, allowing the bleach to penetrate the cortex. Here oxygen released from the peroxide reacts with the natural hair pigments, making them colourless.

Melanin is the pigment that makes the hair black or brown. As the melanin bleaches, the pheomelanin becomes more noticeable. This is the pigment that makes the hair red or yellow. As bleaching proceeds, the hair becomes lighter and lighter, changing through a range of shades – from dark brown, perhaps, through a warm red, to a very pale yellow. The shades and the final colour depend on the proportions of melanin and pheomelanin in the hair.

At some point, the hair stops getting lighter. Some very light brown and blonde hair easily reduces to light shades without toning. With darker hair, though, the final colour after bleaching may still be somewhat yellow. To make it white or platinum, you will need to neutralise any remaining yellow with a toner, usually a violet one.

Overbleaching

Bleaching is a precise process. Too much bleaching will destroy the structure of the hair. Before starting, always process a strand of hair to see how light it will become.

There are several reasons why **overbleaching** may occur:

☆ using peroxide solution that is too strong;
☆ processing the hair for too long;
☆ overlapping hair sections;
☆ combing bleach through previously bleached hair;
☆ bleaching hair that is in poor condition and too porous.

Additionally, if you use a strong peroxide solution and a dryer, the dry heat may increase the speed at which oxygen is produced. This can cause overheating and overprocessing of the hair, making it likely to break.

Even if it doesn't actually break, overbleached hair may

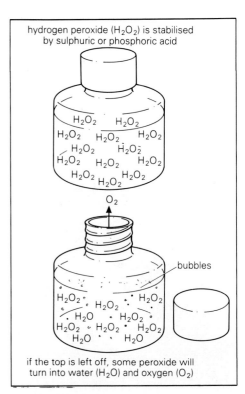

hydrogen peroxide (H_2O_2) is stabilised by sulphuric or phosphoric acid

O_2

bubbles

if the top is left off, some peroxide will turn into water (H_2O) and oxygen (O_2)

Stabilised hydrogen peroxide

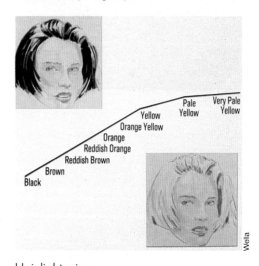

Very Pale Yellow
Pale Yellow
Yellow
Orange Yellow
Orange
Reddish Orange
Reddish Brown
Brown
Black

Wella

Hair lightening

Health and safety

Never use too strong a solution of peroxide. A milder solution applied for longer is kinder to the hair than a stronger one applied for a shorter time.

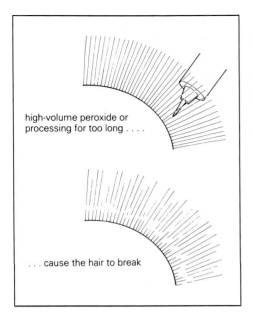

high-volume peroxide or
processing for too long . . . .

. . . cause the hair to break

Overbleaching or over-lightening

Hair bleaches or lighteners

become spongy, very porous, and unevenly coloured. Further colouring, toning or perming become difficult; so does hair management generally. When wet, overbleached hair may resemble chewing gum. The effects of blow-styling and other processes will not last. Even a little tension will break the hair. If the hair gets into this state, you must condition it before processing it chemically in any other way.

Natural bleaching

Sun, wind, sea, sand and chlorinated water affect hair in the same way as bleach. Sun and wind dry and lift the cuticle. Brushing, if sand is present, roughens the cuticle. Hair that has previously been bleached is particularly prone to such effects. Hair exposed to strong **sunlight** is best kept covered; hair exposed to **sea** or **chlorinated water** should be rinsed as soon as possible.

Choosing a bleach process

The client

When a client asks for a bleach process, discuss what she has in mind. You can bleach the whole head, part of the head, or the hair tips only. Or you can make streaks in the hair. Consult with your client as you would for a tint (page 144).

Explain to your client that bleaching, like other chemical processes, affects the condition of the hair. Once you've bleached it your client will need to take special care of the hair at home and return to the salon regularly for further treatment. There will be additional costs in maintaining the effects of bleaching.

Bleaches

Bleaches are supplied as liquids, oils, creams, gels, emulsions, powders and pastes. Each of them needs to be mixed with an oxidant – usually hydrogen peroxide.

☆ **Liquid bleach (simple bleach)** is basically ammonium hydroxide (or 'ammonia'). 1 ml of ammonium hydroxide is mixed with 20–50 ml of hydrogen peroxide. The proportions needed depend on the shade required. If there is too much ammonium hydroxide, the bleach will redden the hair. This mixture lightens the hair by up to three shades.

☆ **Oil bleach** is usually a slightly thicker liquid, containing ammonium hydroxide and sulphonated oils or a thickener. Several types are made. These too are mixed with hydrogen peroxide. They lighten by up to four shades.

☆ **Cream, emulsion and gel bleaches** are thicker substances which contain alkalis (usually ammonium hydroxide), thickening agents, **boosters** or **activators** (which provide additional oxygen), conditioners and other materials. They are mixed with hydrogen peroxide or some other oxidant, and can lighten the hair from dark to light or very light blonde.

☆ **Powder and paste bleaches** are made from magnesium and sodium carbonate. These too are mixed with oxidants, such as hydrogen peroxide, sodium bromate or sodium perborate. The mixture is a creamy paste – probably the thickest of bleach mixes. Ammonium hydroxide or ammonium carbonate is added. These bleaches can lighten hair from dark to very light.

For most modern bleaching requirements the cream or emulsion bleaches and the powder or paste bleaches are the most popular, as these offer a range of lightening.

Using hydrogen peroxide

Hydrogen peroxide may be purchased in the form of a liquid or a cream. It is supplied in different strengths, described in one of two ways. The **volume strength** is the amount of oxygen that the peroxide can produce. For example, 1 litre of '30 volume' peroxide would produce 30 litres of oxygen. The **percentage strength** records how much of the peroxide solution is peroxide, the rest being water. For instance, in 100 g of '9 per cent' or '9%' peroxide there would be 9 g of peroxide and 91 g of water. The strength can be measured with a **peroxometer**.

Bleaching technique

Bleaching all of the hair (virgin hair)

Preparation

☆ Consult your client, examine the hair and scalp, analyse the condition of the hair and so on, as for tinting (page 144).
☆ Make a skin test 48 hours before use, to check your client's reaction to any toner that may be used after bleaching.
☆ Make a test cutting to assess possible results. (This can be taken when the skin test is made.)
☆ Make sure that your client is fully protected with appropriate gowns, towels, etc.
☆ If the hair is greasy or lacquered, shampoo it.

ACTIVITY

Find out how samples of light hair (of the same natural shade) can be bleached using different strengths of bleach.

☆ Prepare the tools, equipment and materials so that they are at hand and ready for use.
☆ Use a barrier cream to protect the client's hairline.
☆ Wear protective gloves or barrier creams to protect your hands.

Sectioning

1 Section the head of hair into four. Sub-divide it into smaller sections as work progresses. Liquid bleaches penetrate easily, so large sections may be taken (about 9–12 mm). For oil bleaches sections should be smaller (about 6–9 mm); for cream and paste bleaches smaller still (about 6 mm or less). As a general guide, use larger sections for thin bleaches and smaller sections for thick bleaches. Hair quantity, too, helps to determine the best section size.
2 Clip the hair well away from the section you are working on.
3 Work methodically, to avoid missing any part of the hair.

Application

1 Mix the bleach so that it is fresh – do not leave it standing.
2 Apply the bleach mixture to the darkest areas first. These are usually around the nape.

    With long hair (approximately 140 mm or more) apply bleach to the mid-lengths first. Leave about 25 mm of the hair tips, and 12–25 mm of the roots, without bleach. Allow the mid-lengths to begin to develop; then apply bleach to the hair tips. When these start developing, apply bleach to the roots. Completely cover all of the hair. This method takes account of the faster development at the roots, due to the heat of the head, and the porosity of the points.

    With short hair (approximately 140 mm or less) apply bleach to the mid-lengths and the ends together. Leave about 12–25 mm of the root ends without bleach. When the mid-lengths and points start to develop, apply bleach to the roots. This method allows for the hair points not being porous.
3 Avoid overlapping previously bleached or over-porous areas. Overlapping could cause overbleaching.
4 Continually apply bleach, working up to the crown area. Complete the application by working on the sides and the top front.
5 When application is complete, check around the hairline, particularly around the ear, for full coverage.
6 Make sure that hair is not packed down. This would prevent air circulating, and slow down processing.

Bleach application: short and long (or virgin) hair

ACTIVITY

Apply bleach to some different hair colour samples. Leave to process for varying times. When developed, rinse the hair. Compare the different degrees of lightness produced by the different times of processing.

Processing

1 Remember that bleach starts developing – releasing oxygen – from the moment it is applied.
2 Carefully time the bleach process. Manufacturers give approximate times, but the process for each client is individual.
3 Make a hair strand colour test from time to time, to check development. Hair looks darker when wet and while you are removing bleach from the hair strand: it will look lighter when dry.
4 If you let the bleach dry out, development will cease.
5 Don't apply heat – this would release the oxygen too fast, resulting in little bleach action.
6 As soon as the strand test indicates the level of lightness required, remove the bleach. Delay at this stage could result in overbleaching.

Bleach removal

1 Use tepid water only. Rinse the bleach from the hair. The scalp may be sensitive, so treat it gently.
2 The hair cuticle may be raised, roughened and easily tangled: take care.
3 When the hair has been thoroughly rinsed, you may apply special conditioners, anti-oxidants or acid balancers to normalise it.
4 Comb the hair correctly – from the points – before blow-styling, setting and shaping it.

Regrowth bleaching

After two or three weeks newly-grown hair will become visible. This regrowth will require bleaching if the colour is to be even.

1 Refer to the client's record for an indication of the development time.
2 Apply the bleach to the regrowth only. Do not allow it to overlap previously bleached hair.
3 Allow processing to continue until the regrowth is bleached to the same level as the rest of the hair.
4 Remove the bleach carefully.
5 Use conditioners, balancers and the like to return the hair to as near normal as possible.

Bleaching some of the hair

The following are some of the terms used to describe bleaching part or parts of the hair: slicing, tipping, blending, streaking,

Regrowth to be bleached

Regrowth bleaching

Tip

Steamers and accelerators supply moist heat and can halve processing times. They may also be used to even out development.

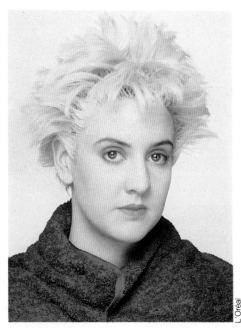

Regrowth bleaching

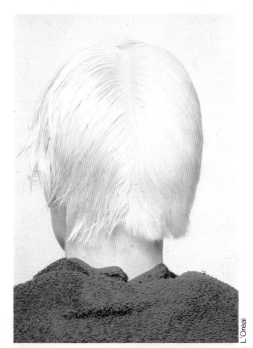

Regrowth newly bleached (*above*)
Hair streaking using a cap (*right*)

weaving, frosting, highlights, lowlights, polishing, brightening, shimmering, and scrunching.

☆ It is usually more effective to lighten small pieces than large, chunky ones.
☆ You can use the more prominent parts of the head to highlight a shape or dressing.
☆ You can use toners to produce varied coloured effects. These may blend with the client's natural colour, or contrast with it.

There are various methods of part bleaching. Especially popular is the use of streaks of lightened hair. Below are two methods of part bleaching.

Streaking

This can be done using a cap:

1 Pull sectioned strands of hair through holes in the plastic cap. (The holes must be carefully positioned.) The cap prevents the bleach running onto other parts of the hair.
2 Apply bleach, using a brush or an applicator.
3 Do not allow the hair to dry out. This would interfere with the bleaching process.
4 You may use a steamer or an accelerator.

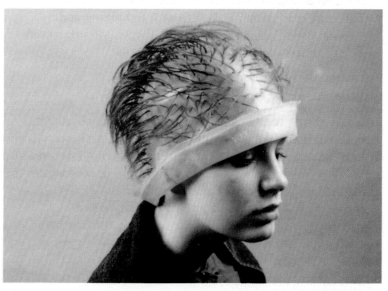

Alternatively, you can use foil:

1 Section small groups of hair strands. Weave or zigzag them so that the hair does not form clumps of lightened or coloured areas.
2 Wrap the sections in aluminium foil, making small packets. The foil retains the heat produced by the oxidants, and the required degree of lightness is reached quickly.

3 Secure the root ends of the strands tightly, to prevent the bleach from running onto them.
4 No heat is necessary. (If you *did* apply heat, the bleach might 'bubble' and run, producing unwanted yellow patches on the roots.)

Part bleaching using foil (*left*)

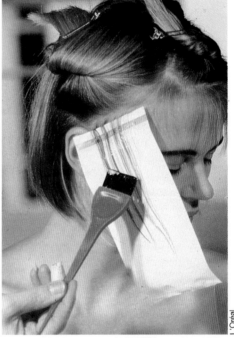

Bleach wraps or **packets** are now made. These are specially designed to cover small sections of hair, or woven hair sections. They seal the hair securely so that the bleach does not run.

There are many other techniques for lightening and bleaching, producing a wide range of effects. Manufacturers of bleach products often suggest methods of use.

Tinting bleached hair

It is easy to tint bleached hair back to a 'natural' colour: it is easier to darken than to lighten. As a client ages, skin and hair colour fade. Resist requests for the 'natural' colour of twenty years ago – the result would probably be too dark. Two or three shades lighter is more likely to be suitable.

If the hair has porous parts, **colour filling** or **pre-pigmentation** is necessary. A base colour in the hair helps other colours to fix more evenly. Red is commonly used. Aim for a warm shade. Ashen, drab and matt shades may show slightly green. Cut off porous ends to allow a normal application.

Successful bleaching

Precautions

☆ Examine the hair and scalp. If there are cuts and abrasions or signs of disease, don't carry out chemical processing.

Part bleaching using Easi-Meche

Part bleaching using Easi-Meche

- ☆ Test the hair for condition, porosity, and tensile strength.
- ☆ Apply bleach materials evenly, at the correct strength.
- ☆ Never overbleach by overlapping, or by processing too long.
- ☆ Never bleach hair coated with metallic or compound hair colourings.
- ☆ Do not allow the bleach to dry. If you do, oxidation will stop.
- ☆ If there is any yellow in the hair after bleaching, apply neutralising shades.
- ☆ On yellow hair, blue colourings or toners may produce green. Test first.
- ☆ Metallic tools and containers may be spoilt if you spill bleach on them. This in turn may cause hair discoloration. Use glass or china containers and measures.
- ☆ Never bleach hair in poor condition or hair that is porous. Overlapping in this case causes the hair to break.
- ☆ Never mix or apply lighteners or colourings without first checking the manufacturer's instructions.
- ☆ Thoroughly remove all traces of bleach materials.
- ☆ Recently bleached hair needs to be treated carefully.
- ☆ After bleaching, neutralise the hair with special conditioners or acid rinses. (The oxidants in bleaches leave the hair somewhat alkaline.)
- ☆ As soon as the bleach has been removed, comb the hair. Comb from the points to the roots. Comb gently, avoiding unnecessary tension.
- ☆ To produce light shades, bleach in stages. When possible, use low peroxide strengths.

Hydrogen peroxide – diluting to the required strength

Strength of peroxide as supplied (%)	Peroxide (parts)		Water (parts)		Strength of peroxide produced (%)
30	3	+	2	→	18
30	2	+	3	→	12
30	3	+	7	→	9
30	1	+	4	→	6
30	1	+	9	→	3
18	2	+	1	→	12
18	1	+	1	→	9
18	1	+	2	→	6
18	1	+	5	→	3
12	3	+	1	→	9
12	1	+	1	→	6
12	1	+	3	→	3

Strength of peroxide as supplied (%)	Peroxide (parts)		Water (parts)		Strength of peroxide produced (%)
9	2	+	1	→	6
9	1	+	2	→	3
6	1	+	1	→	3
3	1	+	2	→	1

Toning

Toning is the process of adding colour, usually to lightened hair. A variety of pastel shades may be used on very light bleached hair. The toner colour range includes beige, silver, rose, and others. Toners give subtle effects. The lightest toners can only be used on the lightest bleached hair. If you use them on dark hair, the colour effect will be lost. Remember that colour added to colour always produces a slightly darker shade. You can mix colours together to produce a wide range. Here are a few examples:

☆ red on green produces brown;
☆ red on yellow produces orange;
☆ blue on yellow produces green;
☆ blue on red produces violet;
☆ violet and orange may be used to neutralise green;
☆ blue may be used to neutralise orange;
☆ violet may be used to neutralise yellow.

The final colour depends both on the depth of the starting hair colour, and on the shades of toners.

Toners may be temporary, semi-permanent, or permanent colourings in a dilute form. There are also specially-made toners for use on lightened hair. These are used like permanent colourings.

Application and processing

The mixing of toners depends on the type used. Those mixed with peroxide need low strengths only. If you use higher strengths you may cause patchy results and porous hair.

Toners are applied in the same way as permanent colourings. Some are poured onto the hair and lightly massaged. All need to be evenly applied, taking into account any porous areas.

Development and processing varies according to the product used. Aniline-derivative toners require 20–45 minutes. Other toners require several applications – colour is only gradually built up in the hair.

Health and safety
Always make skin tests before applying toners.

Faults and corrections

Fault	Possible causes	Correction
Uneven colour	Poor application	Spot-bleach areas as necessary
	Section too large	Recolour
	Incorrect mixing	Prepare a new bleach mixture, combining the ingredients slowly and thoroughly
Dark ends	Under- or overbleached porous ends	Rebleach
	Toner too dark	Remove; use lightener
	Toner overprocessed	Time accurately
	Remains of dark tint	Remove and tone
Too yellow	Underbleached	Bleach lighter
	Base too dark	Try stronger bleach
	Wrong toner used	Use violet
	Wrong bleach	Use a different bleach (*not* an oil bleach)
Too red	Underbleached	Rebleach
	Too much alkali	Use blue bleach (*not* an oil bleach)
	Wrong toner used	Use green, matt, or olive
Dark roots or patches	Poor bleach application	Rebleach, evenly
	Toner too dark	Remove; use lightener
Roots not coloured	Underbleached	Bleach again
	Undertimed	Apply full timing
	'Drippy' toner	Apply cream (*not* liquid)
	Unclean or coated	Clear and re-apply
Colour fade	Overporous	Correct the condition
	Harsh treatment	Advise on hair care
	Exposure	Keep hair covered
	Overprocessed	Comb through only with diluted colour
Hair breakage	Overprocessed	Correct the condition
	Incompatibles	Test
	Harsh treatment	Advise on hair care
	Sleeping in rollers	Demonstrate the effects
Discoloration	Underprocessed	Correct development
	Exposure	Condition hair and cover it
	Home treatments	Test and advise
Green tones	Incompatibles	Test
	Blue on yellow	Use warm or red shades
	Too blue ash	Use violet
Too orange	Overprocessed	Apply blue/ash
	Pigment lacking	Add blue pigment

Fault	Possible causes	Correction
Too yellow	Underprocessed	Add violet
Hair tangled	Overbleached	Use anti-oxidants
	Poor washing	Use correct movements
	Over-rubbing	Use gentle actions
	Backcombing	Reduce and demonstrate
Inflammation	Skin reaction	Seek doctor's advice
	Torn scalp	Seek doctor's advice
	Disease	Seek doctor's advice
Irritation	Skin reaction	Seek doctor's advice
	Harsh treatment	Seek doctor's advice
	Disease	Seek doctor's advice
Colour not taking	Over-porous	Recondition
	Poor condition	Recondition
	Pigment lacking	Pre-pigment
	Lacquer build-up	Remove excess
Colour build-up	Over-porous	Recondition
	Poor condition	Recondition
Hair 'stretchy'	Overprocessed	Treat carefully
	Very porous	Correct the condition
	Very poor condition	Correct the condition
Hair breaking	Overprocessed	Treat carefully
	Overlapping	Correct the condition; restructure
	Combing through too much	Always dilute the tint
	Incompatibles	Test

Decolouring

Decolouring is the removal of colour from the hair – specifically, the removal of synthetic colourings using special **colour reducers** or **strippers**.

☆   Oxidation tints may be removed by **reducing agents**. (Sodium bisulphite and sodium formaldehyde sulphoxylate are two examples.) Most manufacturers make special colour reducers for their products. Whenever possible, use the same make of colour stripper as the colourant.

☆   Avoid oxidants – these tend to help the colour to penetrate, rather than remove it.

☆   Compound henna, vegetable and mineral dyes can only be removed by special colour reducers. Don't use hydrogen peroxide: it is incompatible.

☆   Remove temporary and semi-permanent colourings by repeated washing and the application of spirit.

Application and processing

To remove oxidation dyes and 'para' aniline-derivative dyes from the hair:

1 Wash and dry the hair.
2 Mix the correct colour remover – check the instructions.
3 Apply decolourant to areas to be lightened. Use a brush or a special dispenser.
4 Allow the reducer to act, preferably uncovered and without heat. Processing usually takes 10–30 minutes. With some products, processing can be speeded by covering the hair with a plastic cap and placing it under a warm dryer, steamer or accelerator – follow the manufacturer's instructions.
5 When developed, remove excess chemicals by washing. Normalise the hair. (If you don't do this thoroughly, you will have to repeat the decolouring.)
6 When the decolouring process is complete, make a **'peroxide' test**. This is to check that no synthetic pigment remains. Any remaining synthetic colour will oxidise later and darken again in two or three days. The 'peroxide' test shows whether the decolouring process has been effective. If the hair darkens after testing, remove all chemicals from the test, then re-apply the decolourant. It may take several applications to strip all of the unwanted colour.

Recolouring after decolouring varies according to the products used. In general, do not use any chemical process immediately after decolouring. With some products, however, immediate recolouring is recommended. Perming may be safely carried out, preferably at least a week after decolouring. Where possible perming should be applied *before* decolouring. Consider the lightening action of some normalisers.

How to succeed

Checklist

In preparing for assessments on hair colouring, the following list may be useful. Check that you have covered and fully understood these items:

☐ determining the previous treatments the hair has received;
☐ discussing and selecting suitable colourants;
☐ choosing suitable colour shades, in agreement with the client;
☐ assessing the state of the hair and scalp;
☐ making the necessary skin and hair tests;
☐ sectioning and applying colourants as directed by their suppliers;

- [ ] processing and checking the hair and the client throughout;
- [ ] removing colourants when developed;
- [ ] recording results for future reference.

Self-check quiz

Oral and written questions are used to test your knowledge and understanding. Try the following:

1 Which of the following is the red and yellow pigment?
   (a) melanin
   (b) pheomelanin
   (c) keratin
   (d) carotin

2 Which of the following helps to determine porosity?
   (a) how elastic the hair is
   (b) the cortex
   (c) how hygroscopic the hair is
   (d) the cuticle

3 An allergic skin reaction is indicated by:
   (a) red hair
   (b) colour fade
   (c) a negative reaction
   (d) a positive reaction

Oral test

With the help of a friend, give spoken answers to the following questions:

1 What is hair colouring?
2 What is hair bleaching?
3 What is the chemical process of tinting?
4 What is the chemical process of bleaching?
5 Name the tests that should be made when colouring.
6 Explain each of the following terms:
   (a) virgin hair;
   (b) oxidant;
   (c) skin reaction;
   (d) peroxide.

Written test

Answer the following questions in writing:

1 Consider the technique of permanently colouring.
   (a) How is a suitable colour chosen?
   (b) How is the colourant selected?
   (c) What are the needs and methods of sectioning?

(d) What is the chemical action of the process on hair?

(e) What precautions should be taken?

2 Discuss bleaching.

(a) State what kinds of bleach are used and how they are chosen.

(b) Outline the bleach application.

(c) State the chemical effects on hair structure.

(d) State how 60, 40, and 20 volume peroxide may be diluted to 10 volumes.

(e) State the precautions to be taken.

Kathleen Bray, for Clynol (photo: Ian Hooten)

Normalising

Normalising – principles

Normalising is the process of returning hair to its normal condition after perming. The process is often called **neutralising**, but this word is a little misleading. 'Neutral' describes a chemical state that is neither acidic nor alkaline (pH 7.0). In fact, healthy hair is slightly acidic, so 'normalising' is the more accurate term.

How normalising works

As described in Unit 8, perm lotion acts on the keratin in the hair. The strongest bonds between the polypeptides are the disulphide bridges. Perm lotion breaks some of these, allowing the keratin to take up a new shape. This is how new curls can form.

What normalising does is to make new disulphide bridges. If you didn't normalise the hair, the hair would be weak and likely to break, and the new curls would soon fall out. Normalising is another oxidation process – a process that uses oxygen. Many normalisers contain hydrogen peroxide, but not all. Other oxidants used are sodium bromate and sodium perborate.

Choosing a normaliser

Manufacturers of perm lotions usually produce matching normalisers. These are designed to work together. If possible, always use the normaliser that matches the perm lotion you've used.

A normaliser may be supplied as an emulsion cream, a foam or a liquid. Always follow the manufacturer's instructions. Some can be applied directly from the container, others are applied with a sponge or a brush.

ACTIVITY

Try perm processing with one type of CPW on two or more hair samples or practice blocks. Use a different normaliser for each. Note the different effects, if any.

Normalising technique

Normalising follows directly on from perming. Imagine that you have shampooed, dried and wound the hair. The hair is now perming, and you are timing the perm carefully and making tests to check whether it is complete. You will also be reassuring the client that she has not been forgotten! As soon as the perm is finished, you need to be ready to stop the process immediately.

Preparation

1 Gather together the materials you will need.
2 Make sure there is a washbasin free, preferably one where the client can put her head back to use it. (This makes it easier for you to keep chemicals away from her eyes.)

First rinsing

1 As soon as the perm is complete, move your client immediately to the washbasin. Make sure she is comfortable. Offer her hand towels or tissues in case any liquid trickles over her face.
2 Carefully remove the cap or other head covering. The hair is soft and weak at this stage – don't put unnecessary tension on it. Leave the curlers in place.
3 Run the water. You need an even supply of warm water. The water must be neither hot nor cold. Check the pressure and temperature against the back of your hand. Remember that your client's head may be sensitive after the perming process.
4 Rinse the hair thoroughly with the warm water. This may take about five minutes. It is this rinsing that stops the perm process – until you rinse away the lotion, the hair will still be processing. Direct the water away from the eyes and

Normalising: first rinse (*right*), and towel-drying the hair (*far right*)

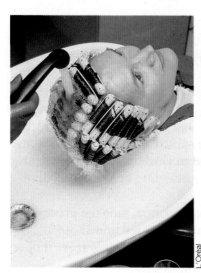

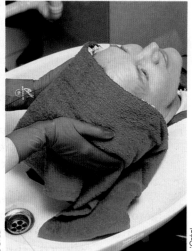

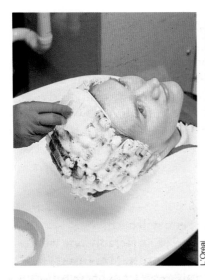
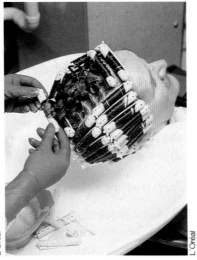
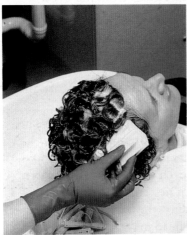

Normalising: first application (*above left*); removing curlers (*above*); second application of normaliser (*left*)

the face. Make sure you rinse all of the hair, including the nape curlers. If a curler slips out, gently wind the hair back onto it immediately.

Applying normaliser

1 Raise your client to a comfortable sitting position.
2 Blot the hair thoroughly, using a towel or tissues. It may help if you pack the curlers with cottonwool.
3 When there is no surplus water, apply the normaliser. Follow the manufacturer's instructions. These may tell you to pour the normaliser through the hair, or apply it with a brush or sponge, or use the spiked applicator bottle. Some foam normalisers need to be pushed briskly into the hair. Make sure that normaliser comes into contact with all of the hair.
4 When all of the hair has been covered, time the process according to the instructions. The usual time is 5–10 minutes. You may wrap the hair in a towel or leave it open to the air – follow the instructions.

ACTIVITY

Collect together several hair samples. Wind and process each with CPW. Follow the manufacturer's instructions. Apply normaliser to each sample. Process the normaliser, allowing 5, 10, 15 and 20 minutes and longer. Compare the results. Record the effects produced by the different normalising times.

5 Gently and carefully remove the curlers. Don't pull or stretch the hair. The hair may still be soft, especially towards the ends.

6 Apply the normaliser to the hair again, covering all of the hair. Arrange the hair so that the normaliser does not run over the face. Leave for the time recommended, perhaps another 5–10 minutes.

Second rinsing

1 Run the water, again checking temperature and pressure.
2 Rinse the hair thoroughly to remove the normaliser.
3 You can now treat the hair with an after-perm aid or conditioner. Use the one recommended by the manufacturer of the perm and normaliser, to be sure that the chemicals are compatible.

ACTIVITY

With CPW hair samples, try using different volume strengths of hydrogen peroxide in the normaliser. Compare the effects.

> **Tip**
>
> Remove end wraps from the curlers after use. Rinse, dry and powder the curlers. This prevents the rubbers from becoming soft. Separate the curlers into different sizes and colours, ready for the next use.

Successful normalising

At the end of the normalising process, you will have returned the hair to a normal, stable state.

☆ The reduction and oxidation processes will have been completed.

☆ Finishing aids or conditioners (anti-oxidants) may need to be applied to counteract the oxidants used.

☆ The hair will now be slightly weaker – fewer bonds will have formed than were broken by the perm. Special conditioners may be needed. If the cuticle is lifting or roughened, this too may be countered with conditioners.

☆ Record any hair or perm faults on the client's record card. Correct faults as appropriate.

☆ **Under-normalising** – not leaving normaliser on for long enough – results in a slack curl or waves.

☆ **Over-oxidising** – leaving the normaliser on too long or using oxidants that are too strong – results in salt bonds. These are not as strong as disulphide linkages, so the curl will rapidly fall.

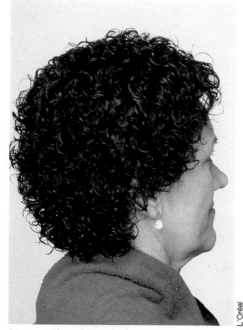

Hair ready to be styled

The hair should be ready for shaping, blow-drying or setting.

How to succeed

Checklist

In preparing for assessments on normalising, the following list may be useful. Check that you have covered and fully understood these items:

- [ ] checking that the perm has taken, by testing the curl achieved;
- [ ] understanding the oxidation process of neutralising;
- [ ] outlining perm effects on hair structure;
- [ ] carrying out the normalising process;
- [ ] using after-perm conditioners or other products as instructed;
- [ ] finishing normalising as required by the manufacturers;
- [ ] preparing hair for after-perm services;
- [ ] stating how the normaliser works;
- [ ] discussing after-perm care with clients.

Self-check quiz

Oral and written questions are used to test your knowledge and understanding. Try the following:

1 The process of normalising is one of:
   (a) polymerisation
   (b) keratinisation
   (c) reduction
   (d) oxidation

2 Before normalising, make sure that the CPW lotion is:
   (a) dried
   (b) heated
   (c) rinsed
   (d) cooled

3 In normalising oxygen joins with the following to form water:
   (a) carbon
   (b) sulphur
   (c) hydrogen
   (d) nitrogen

Oral test

With the help of a friend, give spoken answers to the following questions:

1 When should normaliser be used?
2 Which chemical is most commonly used in normalising?
3 Why is the timing of the normalising process important?

4 State some precautions to be taken when normalising.

5 Describe the process of normalising.

Written test

Answer the following questions in writing:

1 With regard to normalising:
    (a) state what normalising is and does;
    (b) describe the relevant physical factors;
    (c) describe the relevant chemical factors;
    (d) state what over-normalising is and does;
    (e) list the most important points of normalising.

2 Describe the effects of normalisation. State:
    (a) why it is necessary;
    (b) what chemicals are involved;
    (c) the effects on the keratin structure;
    (d) the different oxidants used;
    (e) the safety factors involved.

Selling in the salon

Selling – principles

Clients visiting the salon do so in order to make a purchase – they come to buy your hairdressing services. What you offer is not merely the practical work you do, but also your experience and advice. You are therefore in the business of **selling**: your skills, the materials you use, and perhaps products to take away for home use. In the salon you can offer individual attention and **expertise** in hair care beyond what is available in stores and supermarkets.

The salon needs income, to pay running costs – including your wages. This income comes from sales to clients. The salon will welcome a growing number of regular clients, clients who keep coming back because they are satisfied with what they bought last time. This is why your selling technique needs to be effective.

> **Tip**
> Never be aggressive in your selling. You may succeed in selling on that occasion, but the salon will probably lose a client.

Hairdressing services

Services consist of all the practical skills you offer – cutting, styling, perming, tinting, and so on. The client will notice not just whether you are **competent** in these, but *how* you carry them out. For example, are you welcoming? Do you remember your client's name? Do you explain at each stage what you're going to do, and how long it's likely to take? Are you tactful but honest? Do you give helpful advice about hair care at home?

In many salons it is only the hairdressing services that are

> **ACTIVITY**
> Make lists of all the hairdressing services, service materials used, and retail goods that could usefully be offered for sale in the salon.

offered for sale. In some, though, other services may be available, such as manicure or beauty treatments.

Materials and equipment

The materials and equipment you use – the shampoos, perm lotions, hair tints, curlers, hairdryers and the like – should be chosen for quality, reliability, effectiveness and safety. Good manufacturers invest a great deal of money in researching and testing their products. They also spend a lot on **advertising**, some aimed at people who work in the hairdressing trade, much of it at clients. They provide instructions for the use of their products, and leaflets illustrating how they work and what they can do. **Packaging**, too, is used to make the products attractive.

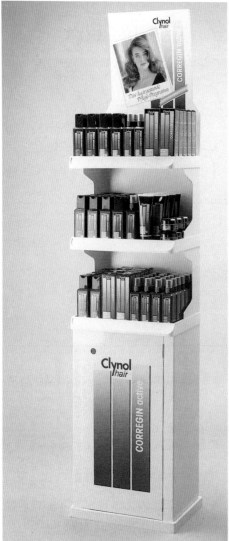

> ### *Health and safety*
>
> Always read instructions thoroughly – don't just assume that you know how to use a product. Correct use is vital if you are to achieve the best possible result and to avoid health risks to yourself and your clients.

Retail products

Apart from the products you use in the salon, you may have products to sell to clients for home use. Some examples:

☆ **cosmetics**, such as shampoos, hair sprays, or perfumes;
☆ **equipment**, such as blow-dryers, hot brushes, curlers, or shavers;
☆ **hair accessories**, such as clips, pins, combs, brushes, hair ornaments, or postiche;
☆ **dress accessories**, such as brooches, earrings, stick pins, scarves, shawls, or handkerchiefs.

Products such as these need to be attractively displayed where the client will see them.

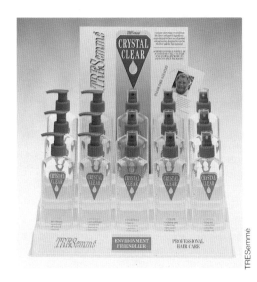

Selling technique

To sell effectively, you need to know what it is you are selling, and whether or not it is suitable for the client. Here are some guidelines:

☆ Make sure you are able to describe the product – what it is, and how it should be used. Personal experience is a great help in this.
☆ Make sure you can discuss both the advantages and any disadvantages of this product. Is there a similar product that might be better?
☆ Make clear to the client what the product will cost. In some cases the costs will include not just the initial purchase but special materials for use afterwards. For example, some hair shampoos need to be followed up with special conditioners, and then hairsprays – all from the same manufacturer.
☆ If the product is a piece of equipment, how long is it likely to last? If the product is an effect (such as temporary hair colour), how long is the effect likely to last?
☆ Discuss possible purchases with your client. Don't recommend something if you really think it's unsuitable.
☆ When you have agreed on the purchase, check that the client understands how to use the product at home.

Next time the client visits the salon, you might like to ask whether she was pleased with what she bought. Clients are always glad of such personal attention. Also, your question may bring to light problems in use: you may be able to offer help in solving these.

The client

There is no need to overwhelm your client with products available for purchase, or repeat the list each time she visits the salon. At some point the opportunity will arise naturally out of your discussion.

ACTIVITY

Visit your local bank and find out about banking services, both for you as an individual and for the salon. If you don't already have one, find out how to open a bank account and the advantages of having one. Make sure you know how cheques are correctly written and what to check when you are given one.

☆ Discuss with your client her needs and expectations. These may influence how much she is willing to spend on hairdressing products.

☆ Questions may be helpful in identifying problems and products that may solve them. 'Are you having any difficulties with your hair?' 'Is your hair always as dry as this?' 'How long does your blow-style last?' 'Do you want a particular kind of perm?'

☆ As you consult with your client, you may need to offer advice about additional work that is needed. For example, the client may propose a shampoo and blow-style, but it may seem to you that the hair needs also to be cut and shaped if the style is to look good. You now need to 'sell' the additional service of cutting and shaping.

☆ Always indicate to clients how long services will take, and how long they will be in the salon.

☆ Make clear to the client what services and products will cost. Display a price list where they can easily see it.

☆ At the end of your discussion, check that you and your client are agreed about what is to be done. Offer a summary of the action you have agreed upon.

☆ If appropriate, offer suggestions about after-care and products that would help in this.

Tip

Clients cannot choose unless they know what is available. Always make clear the range of products and services you are offering.

Characteristics

By listening to your client and observing her carefully you will get to know her **characteristics**. These indicate what she might want to purchase.

☆ *The client's age* indicates specific styles that may be worn, and products that may be used.

☆ *The client's status and position* may indicate how often styling is needed. For example, she may be concerned about her appearance at work.

☆ *The way the client dresses*, the choice of colours worn, and the quality afforded, indicate how adventurous she is and what her finances will allow.

☆ *The frequency of salon visits* indicates whether products are needed for home use. There may also be family needs.

☆ *The client's natural colouring* indicates suitable hair colours and skin cosmetics.

☆ *The client's facial shapes and features* indicate styles that would be practical and suitable.

Interest

Clients often indicate their interest in purchasing services or goods. Learn to look for the signals, as these may lead to sales if you are ready to respond promptly. Here are some examples:

- ☆ The client admires a style in a book or on another person.
- ☆ She expresses dislike of own natural hair colour.
- ☆ She expresses satisfaction with salon products used previously.
- ☆ She wonders aloud what home products there are to use.
- ☆ She comments on the perfume, colour or look of a product.
- ☆ She looks at and handles goods.
- ☆ She complains of scalp problems or hair difficulties.
- ☆ She seeks advice on what home-use equipment is available.
- ☆ Her hair or skin looks in need of attention.

ACTIVITY

Look in the local public or college libraries for books on social psychology, personal relationships, and selling. There are now several interesting books on body language.

Image

The way in which clients see hairdressers is important. Clients will be favourably impressed with hairdressers who display enthusiasm, conscientiousness, good taste and reliability. These qualities are reassuring.

In order to gain clients' confidence, hairdressers need to present themselves in a way that merits it. Here are a few useful hints. If you observe these, you may motivate your clients to make purchases from you:

- ☆ **Appearance and general manner** These affect how the client views you. Your own choice of hairstyle, make-up, fashion clothes and colour will be seen as examples.
- ☆ **Personal care** Cleanliness and personal hygiene are essential. They concern not only how you look but everyone else's health.
- ☆ **Deportment** The way you stand and the way you walk indicate to clients the care you take in your work.
- ☆ **Competence** The skills you offer should be of a high professional standard. Aim to give satisfaction to clients. Professional certification, together with practical experience, will lead to satisfied clients who return to your salon and ask for *your* services.
- ☆ **General behaviour** If you are courteous and polite, clients will notice and appreciate this. They will be more likely to buy products and services from those who offer care and consideration.
- ☆ **Personal relationships** Clients will feel more comfortable in a salon where they have a good relationship with the hairdresser, and where the staff get on well with each other. The **non-verbal signs** of body language and eye contact are important here.
- ☆ **Speech** What you say and the way you put it are most important. Being able to communicate is essential. Choose your words with care. Accents and dialects are usually popular and distinctive – there is no need to disguise these.

City and Guilds
of London Institute

HAIRDRESSING
Training
B O A R D

City & Guilds of London Institute

City and Guilds
of London Institute

HAIRDRESSING
Training
B O A R D

City & Guilds of London Institute

> ### *Tip*
> How you look, present yourself, act, move and speak all make an impression of some kind on those you meet. Try always to make the right impression: of being competent, trustworthy and friendly.

Successful selling

☆ Display, present and offer your products, both services and goods.

☆ Gain your client's attention.

☆ Outline what the products can do.

☆ Offer professional advice and guidance.

☆ Allow the client to consider, without hurrying her.

☆ Follow up the sale – determine the sizes, quantities or types required.

☆ Summarise and confirm the purchase and the cost.

☆ Close the sale by taking the payment.

☆ Present the wrapped goods and a receipt.

☆ Record the service or sale, so that stock can be replaced.

☆ Ask the client when she would like her next appointment to be.

ACTIVITY

Collect information on the various bank cards, from banks, post offices, building societies, and elsewhere.

How to succeed

Checklist

In preparing for assessments on selling, the following list may be useful. Check that you have covered and fully understood these items:

- [ ] your general approach to the client;
- [ ] your method of gaining information (questioning techniques);
- [ ] your choice and selection of products to meet the client's needs;
- [ ] your presentation of products for sale;
- [ ] the clarity of your description of products;
- [ ] your follow-up and closing of the sale;
- [ ] the efficiency of your conduct throughout;
- [ ] the satisfaction or other reactions displayed by the client.

Self-check quiz

Oral and written questions are used to test your knowledge and understanding. Try the following:

1 The hairdresser can offer the following:
   - (a) loans
   - (b) expertise
   - (c) hire purchase
   - (d) medical treatment

2 The following is one of the salon's products for sale:
   - (a) a chair
   - (b) a mirror
   - (c) a shower
   - (d) a hairstyle

3 Product differences between service materials need to be:
   - (a) used
   - (b) bought
   - (c) described
   - (d) sold

Oral test

With the help of a friend, give spoken answers to the following questions:

1 Give an example of a question to be asked of a prospective buyer.
2 Describe three aspects of selling.
3 Name some signals that may indicate willingness to buy.
4 Why should sales and services be recorded?

5 What are the products for sale in your salon?

Written test

Answer the following questions in writing:

1 Consider sales in the salon.
  (a) Describe the products that may be available.
  (b) Outline one salon product.
  (c) Outline some client characteristics which might indicate readiness to make purchases in the salon.
  (d) Describe how clients' needs can be determined.
  (e) List the points of selling.

2 Think about the technique of selling:
  (a) List suitable questions that would be useful in determining clients' needs.
  (b) List signals from clients which indicate their interest in making purchases.
  (c) Outline aspects of hairdressers themselves which might encourage sales.
  (d) Outline the services offered by the salon.
  (e) State why salons might be better able to meet clients' needs than hairdressers working at clients' homes.

ANSWERS TO SELF-CHECK QUIZZES

Unit 1 (page 15): 1 (c) 2 (b) 3 (a); Unit 2 (page 40): 1 (c) 2 (d) 3 (b); Unit 3 (page 54): 1 (d) 2 (c) 3 (c); Unit 4 (page 65): 1 (b) 2 (b) 3 (a); Unit 5 (page 88): 1 (c) 2 (b) 3 (b); Unit 6 (page 97): 1 (b) 2 (c) 3 (c); Unit 7 (page 118): 1 (c) 2 (c) 3 (c); Unit 8 (page 137): 1 (c) 2 (a) 3 (b); Unit 9 (page 168): 1 (b) 2 (d) 3 (d); Unit 10 (page 174): 1 (d) 2 (c) 3 (c); Unit 11 (page 182): 1 (b) 2 (d) 3 (c).

RECOMMENDED READING

Almond, Elaine 1986. *Safety in the Salon*. Stanley Thornes.

Bennett, Ruth 1984. *The Science of Hairdressing*. Edward Arnold.

Boston, M. and N. Bloomfield 1974. *How to Blow Style*. Permaids Products Ltd.

Browne, Ginger 1990. *Afro Hair – Procedures & Techniques*. Stanley Thornes.

Coen, P., J. Maxwell and J. Wagenvoord 1988. *Beautiful Braids*. Century Hutchinson/Random House.

Cutting, P., R. Ross and R. Hill 1991. *Hairdressing – Theory, Science and Practice*. Pitman.

Galvin, Joshua and Daniel 1985. *Hair Matters*. Macmillan Education.

Hatton, Lesley and Phillip Hatton 1990. *Foundation Hairdressing*. BSP Professional Books.

Hatton, Lesley, Phillip Hatton and Alisoun Powell 1987. *Salon Handbook* Series. BSP Professional Books.

Henderson, S. 1991. *Basic Hairdressing*. Stanley Thornes.

Henderson, S. and M. Phillips 1988. *Hairdressing and Science*. Stanley Thornes.

Jackson, Barbara and Lydia Eagle 1984. *The Black Book of Beauty*. Macmillan.

Jarrett, Hyacinth 1988. *The Black Hairdressing & Beauty Training Manual*. Manpower Services Commission.

Kilgour, O. F. G. and Marguerite McGarry 1984. *Complete Hairdressing Science*. Heinemann.

Lee, C. N. and J. K. Inglis 1983. *Science for Hairdressing Students*. Pergamon.

Mascola, Anthony 1988. *Hairstyling*. Toni and Guy.

Masters, T. W. 1984. *Hairdressing in Theory and Practice*. Technical Press.

Openshaw, F. 1986. *Hairdressing Science*. Longman.

Palladino, Leo 1984. *Mastering Hairdressing*. Macmillan Education.

Palladino, Leo 1989. *Principles and Practice of Hairdressing*. Macmillan Education.

Peberdy, W. G. 1988. *Sterilization and Hygiene*. Stanley Thornes.

Sassoon, Vidal 1984. *Cutting Hair the Vidal Sassoon Way*. Heinemann.

Young, Marc 1979. *Creative Haircutting My Way*. Marc Young Artistes de Coiffeur Ltd.

INDEX